PATIENT CARE UNDER UNCERTAINTY

Patient Care under Uncertainty

Charles F. Manski

PRINCETON UNIVERSITY PRESS

PRINCETON AND OXFORD

Copyright © 2019 by Princeton University Press

Published by Princeton University Press
41 William Street, Princeton, New Jersey 08540
6 Oxford Street, Woodstock, Oxfordshire OX20 1TR

press.princeton.edu

All Rights Reserved

Library of Congress Cataloging-in-Publication Data

Names: Manski, Charles F., author.
Title: Patient care under uncertainty / Charles F. Manski.
Description: Princeton : Princeton University Press, [2019] |
    Includes bibliographical references and index.
Identifiers: LCCN 2019018775 | ISBN 9780691194738 (hardback : alk. paper)
Subjects: | MESH: Evidence-Based Medicine—economics | Uncertainty | Clinical
    Decision-Making | Quality of Health Care—economics | Economics, Medical
Classification: LCC RA410 | NLM WB 102.5 | DDC 338.4/73621—dc23
    LC record available at https://lccn.loc.gov/2019018775

ISBN (e-book) 978-0-691-19473-8

British Library Cataloging-in-Publication Data is available

Editorial: Joe Jackson and Jaqueline Delaney
Production Editorial: Brigitte Pelner
Jacket/Cover Design: Layla Mac Rory
Production: Erin Suydam
Publicity: Nathalie Levine (U.S.) and Julia Hall (U.K.)
Copyeditor: Karen Verde

This book has been composed in Adobe Text and Gotham

Printed on acid-free paper ∞

Printed in the United States of America

10 9 8 7 6 5 4 3 2 1

*To Drs. William Berenberg, Sunandana Chandra, Henry Hashkes,
Timothy Kuzel, Neill Peters, Byron Starr, and Jeffrey Wayne*

CONTENTS

PREFACE

I can date the onset of my professional concern with patient care under uncertainty to the late 1990s, when I initiated research that led to a co-authored article re-assessing the findings of a randomized trial comparing treatments for hypertension. Since then I have increasingly used patient care to illustrate broad methodological issues in analysis of treatment response and I have increasingly studied specific aspects of patient care.

I can date the onset of my personal interest in the subject to 1985, when I became seriously ill with fever and weakness while on a major trip to Europe and Israel. After a difficult period where I pushed myself to give lectures in Helsinki and attend a conference in Paris, I arrived in Jerusalem and essentially collapsed. I was hospitalized for several days at the Hadassah Hospital on Mt. Scopus, but my symptoms did not suggest a diagnosis. When I had the opportunity to see my medical chart, I found the designation "FUO." I asked an attending physician to explain this term and learned that it is an acronym for "fever of unknown origin." I was thus introduced to medical uncertainty. (A month later, after returning home to Madison, Wisconsin, I was diagnosed with Lyme disease and treated successfully with antibiotics. Lyme disease was then relatively new to the United States. It had apparently never been observed in Israel prior to my case.)

While writing this book, I benefited from helpful comments on draft chapters provided by Matt Masten, Ahmad von Schlegell, Shaun Shaikh, and Bruce Spencer. I also benefited from the opportunity to lecture on the material to interdisciplinary audiences of researchers at McMaster University and Duke University.

As the writing progressed, I increasingly appreciated the care that I have received from dedicated clinicians throughout my life. The book is dedicated to some of these persons, a small expression of my gratitude.

PATIENT CARE UNDER UNCERTAINTY

Introduction

There are three broad branches of decision analysis: normative, descriptive, and prescriptive. Normative analysis seeks to establish ideal properties of decision making, often aiming to give meaning to the terms "optimal" and "rational." Descriptive analysis seeks to understand and predict how actual decision makers behave. Prescriptive analysis seeks to improve the performance of actual decision making.

One might view normative and descriptive analysis as entirely distinct subjects. It is not possible, however, to cleanly separate prescriptive analysis from the other branches of study. Prescriptive analysis aims to improve actual decisions, so it must draw on normative thinking to define "improve" and on descriptive research to characterize actual decisions.

This book offers prescriptive analysis that seeks to improve patient care. My focus is decision making under uncertainty regarding patient health status and response to treatment. By "uncertainty," I do not just mean that clinicians and health planners may make probabilistic rather than definite predictions of patient outcomes. My main concern is decision making when the available evidence and medical knowledge do not suffice to yield precise probabilistic predictions.

For example, an educated patient who is comfortable with probabilistic thinking may ask her clinician a seemingly straightforward question such as "What is the chance that I will develop disease X in the next five years?" or "What is the chance that treatment Y will cure me?" Yet the clinician may not be able to provide precise answers to these questions. A credible response may be a range, say "20 to 40 percent" or "at least 50 percent."

Decision theorists use the terms "deep uncertainty" and "ambiguity" to describe the decision settings I address, but I shall encompass them within the broader term "uncertainty" for now. Uncertainty in patient care is common and has sometimes been acknowledged verbally. For example, the Evidence-Based Medicine Working Group asserts that (Institute of Medicine, 2011, p. 33): "clinicians must accept uncertainty and the notion that clinical decisions are often made with scant knowledge of their true impact." However, uncertainty has generally not been addressed in research on evidence-based medicine, which has been grounded in classical statistical theory. I think this a huge omission, which this book strives to correct.

Surveillance or Aggressive Treatment

I pay considerable attention to the large class of decisions that choose between surveillance and aggressive treatment of patients at risk of potential disease. Consider, for example, women at risk of breast cancer. In this instance, surveillance typically means undergoing periodic mammograms and clinical exams, while aggressive treatment may mean preventive drug treatment or mastectomy.

Other familiar examples are choice between surveillance and drug treatment for patients at risk of heart disease or diabetes. Yet others are choice between surveillance and aggressive treatment of patients who have been treated for localized cancer and are at risk of metastasis. A semantically distinct but logically equivalent decision is choice between diagnosis of patients as healthy or ill. With diagnosis, the concern is not to judge whether a patient will develop a disease in the future but whether the patient is currently ill and requires treatment.

These decisions are common, important to health, and familiar to clinicians and patients alike. Indeed, patients make their own choices related to surveillance and aggressive treatment. They perform self-surveillance by monitoring their own health status. They choose how faithfully to adhere to surveillance schedules and treatment regimens prescribed by clinicians.

Uncertainty often looms large when a clinician contemplates choice between surveillance and aggressive treatment. The effectiveness of surveillance in mitigating the risk of disease may depend on the degree to which a patient will adhere to the schedule of clinic visits prescribed in a surveillance plan. Aggressive treatment may be more beneficial than surveillance to the extent that it reduces the risk of disease development or the severity of disease that does develop. It may be more harmful to the extent that it generates health side effects and financial costs beyond those associated with surveillance. There often is substantial uncertainty about all these matters.

Evolution of the Book

I am an economist with specialization in econometrics. I have no formal training in medicine. One may naturally ask how I developed an interest in patient care under uncertainty and feel able to contribute to the subject. It would be arrogant and foolhardy for me to dispense medical advice regarding specific aspects of patient care. I will not do so. The contributions that I feel able to make concern the methodology of evidence-based medicine. This matter lies within the expertise of econometricians, statisticians, and decision analysts.

Research on treatment response and risk assessment shares a common objective: probabilistic prediction of patient outcomes given knowledge of observed patient attributes. Development of methodology for prediction of outcomes conditional on observed attributes has long been a core concern of many academic disciplines.

Econometricians and statisticians commonly refer to conditional prediction as *regression*, a term in use since the nineteenth century. Some psychologists have used the terms *actuarial prediction* and *statistical prediction*. Computer scientists may refer to *machine learning* and *artificial intelligence*. Researchers in business schools may speak of *predictive analytics*. All these terms are used to describe methods that have been developed to enable conditional prediction.

As an econometrician, I have studied how statistical imprecision and identification problems affect empirical (or evidence-based) research that uses sample data to predict population outcomes. Statistical theory characterizes the imprecise inferences that can be drawn about the outcome distribution in a study population by observing the outcomes of a finite sample of its members. Identification problems are inferential difficulties that persist even when sample size grows without bound.

A classic example of statistical imprecision occurs when one draws a random sample of a population and uses the sample average of an outcome to estimate the population mean outcome. Statisticians typically measure imprecision of the estimate by its variance, which decreases to zero as sample size increases. Whether imprecision is measured by variance or another way, the famous "Laws of Large Numbers" imply that imprecision vanishes as sample size increases.

Identification problems encompass the spectrum of issues that are sometimes called *non-sampling errors* or *data-quality problems*. These issues cannot be resolved by amassing so-called big data. They may be mitigated by collecting better data, but not by merely collecting more data.

A classic example of an identification problem is generated by missing data. Suppose that one draws a random sample of a population, but one observes only some sample outcomes. Increasing sample size adds new observations, but it also yields further missing data. Unless one learns the values of the missing data or knows the process that generates missing data, one cannot precisely learn the population mean outcome as sample size increases.

My research has focused mainly on identification problems, which often are the dominant difficulty in empirical research. I have studied probabilistic prediction of outcomes when available data are combined with relatively weak assumptions that have some claim to credibility. While much of this work has necessarily been technical, I have persistently stressed the simple truth that research cannot yield decision-relevant findings based on evidence alone.

In Manski (2013a) I observed that the logic of empirical inference is summarized by the relationship:

$$\text{assumptions} + \text{data} \Rightarrow \text{conclusions}.$$

Data (or evidence) alone do not suffice to draw useful conclusions. Inference also requires assumptions (or theories, hypotheses, premises, suppositions) that relate the data to the population of interest. Holding fixed the available data, and presuming avoidance of errors in logic, stronger assumptions yield stronger conclusions. At the extreme, one may achieve certitude by posing sufficiently strong assumptions. A fundamental difficulty of empirical research is to decide what assumptions to maintain.

Strong conclusions are desirable, so one may be tempted to maintain strong assumptions. I have emphasized that there is a tension between the strength of assumptions and their credibility, calling this (Manski, 2003, p. 1):

The Law of Decreasing Credibility: The credibility of inference decreases with the strength of the assumptions maintained.

This "Law" implies that analysts face a dilemma as they decide what assumptions to maintain: Stronger assumptions yield conclusions that are more powerful but less credible.

I have argued against making precise probabilistic predictions with *incredible certitude*. It has been common for experts to assert that some event will occur with a precisely stated probability. However, such predictions often are fragile, resting on unsupported assumptions and limited data. Thus, the expressed certitude is not credible.

Motivated by these broad ideas, I have studied many prediction problems and have repeatedly found that empirical research may be able to credibly bound the probability that an event will occur but not make credible precise probabilistic predictions, even with large data samples. In econometrics jargon, probabilities of future events may be *partially identified* rather than *point identified*. This work, which began in the late 1980s, has been published in numerous journal articles and synthesized in multiple books, written at successive stages of my research program and at technical levels suitable for different audiences (Manski, 1995, 2003, 2005, 2007a, 2013a).

Whereas my early research focused on probabilistic prediction per se, I have over time extended its scope to study decision making under uncertainty; that is, decisions when credible precise probabilistic predictions are not available. Thus, my research has expanded from econometrics to prescriptive decision analysis.

Elementary decision theory suggests a two-step process for choice under uncertainty. Considering the feasible alternatives, the first step is to eliminate dominated actions—an action is dominated if one knows for sure that some other action is superior. The second step is to choose an undominated action. This is subtle because there is no consensus regarding the optimal way to choose among undominated alternatives. There are only various reasonable ways. I will later give content to the word "reasonable."

Decision theory is mathematically rigorous, but it can appear sterile when presented in abstraction. The subject comes alive when applied to important actual decision problems. I have studied various public and private decisions under uncertainty. This work has yielded technical research articles and a book on public policy under uncertainty written for a broad audience (Manski, 2013a).

I have increasingly felt that patient care is ripe for study as a problem of decision making under uncertainty. I therefore have sought to learn enough about research on evidence-based medicine to make original contributions that build on my methodological background in econometrics and decision analysis. The results include studies of diagnostic testing and treatment under uncertainty (Manski, 2009, 2013b), personalized care with partial assessment of health risks (Manski, 2018a), analysis and design of randomized clinical trials (Manski, 2004a; Manski and Tetenov, 2016, 2019), drug approval (Manski, 2009), and vaccination policy with partial knowledge of disease transmission (Manski, 2010, 2017). I have also written a review article (Manski, 2018b).

The idea of writing a book evolved as I have accumulated background in evidence-based medicine and have developed an enlarging set of original research findings. A book provides the space to present major themes and to show how they become manifest in various contexts. A book enables an author to speak to a broader audience than is possible when writing research articles on particular topics.

I hope that this book will prove useful to a spectrum of readers. I would like it to help clinicians and public health planners recognize and cope with uncertainty as they make decisions about patient care. It may help patients to become informed about and participate in their own care. I anticipate that the book will help medical researchers design randomized trials and interpret the evidence they obtain from trials and observational studies. I will be pleased if the book encourages the biostatisticians who assist medical researchers to make constructive use of modern methodological advances in econometrics and statistical decision theory.

Some readers with certain types of expertise will correctly view the book as critical of the methodologies they have advocated. These include biostatisticians who have used the statistical theory of hypothesis testing to advise medical researchers on the design and analysis of randomized trials. They include personnel at the US Food and Drug Administration and other governmental agencies who regulate approval of new drugs, biologics, and medical devices. They include developers of clinical practice guidelines who have argued that evidence-based medicine should rest either solely or predominately on evidence from randomized trials, disregarding or downplaying evidence from observational studies. I hope that these readers will make the effort to understand the bases for my criticisms and that they will view the prescriptive decision analysis presented here as constructive suggestions.

Summary

Aiming to make the book accessible to a wide readership, the exposition in the main text is almost entirely verbal rather than mathematical. For readers who want to dig deeper, I include a set of complements that formalize or elaborate on key parts of the discussion in the main text. I also provide references to the technical articles that present the full analysis.

The eight chapters of the book move from review and critique in chapters 1 and 2 to prescription in chapters 3 through 7 and conclusion. Chapter 1 reviews the continuing discourse in medicine regarding the circumstances in which clinicians should adhere to evidence-based practice guidelines or exercise their own judgment, sometimes called "expert opinion." Chapter 2 critiques how evidence from randomized trials has been used to inform medical decision making.

Chapter 3 describes research on identification, whose aim is credible use of evidence to inform patient care. Chapter 4 develops decision-theoretic principles for reasonable care under uncertainty. Chapter 5 considers reasonable decision making with sample data from randomized trials. Moving away from consideration of a clinician treating an individual patient, chapter 6 views patient care from a population health perspective. Chapter 7 considers management of uncertainty in drug approval. The final chapter provides concluding suggestions that encourage putting the themes of the book into practice.

1

Clinical Guidelines and Clinical Judgment

1.1. Adherence to Guidelines or Exercise of Judgment?

Medical textbooks and training have long offered clinicians guidance in patient care. Such guidance has increasingly become institutionalized through issuance of clinical practice guidelines (CPGs). The material made available by the National Guideline Clearinghouse at Agency for Healthcare Research and Quality (2017) gives a sense of the current scale and scope. Until 2018, the Clearinghouse provided periodically updated summaries of several thousand evidence-based guidelines issued by numerous health organizations.

Dictionaries typically define a "guideline" as a suggestion or advice for behavior rather than a mandate. Two among many definitions of CPGs are given by Hoyt (1997) and Institute of Medicine (IOM) (2011). Hoyt writes that CPGs are

> official statements of practice groups, hospitals, organizations, or agencies regarding proper management of a specific clinical problem or the proper indications for performing a procedure or treatment. (1997, p. 32)

The IOM committee writes:

> Clinical practice guidelines are statements that include recommendations intended to optimize patient care that are informed by a systematic

review of evidence and an assessment of the benefits and harms of alternative care options. (2011, p. 4)

Neither Hoyt nor the IOM committee define CPGs as mandates. However, clinicians may have strong incentives to comply with guidelines, making adherence sometimes close to compulsory. A patient's health insurance plan may require adherence to a CPG as a condition for reimbursement of the cost of treatment. Adherence may furnish evidence of due diligence that legally defends a clinician in the event of a malpractice claim. Less dramatically, adherence to guidelines provides a rationale for care decisions that might otherwise be questioned by patients, colleagues, or employers.

The medical literature contains many commentaries exhorting clinicians to adhere to guidelines, arguing that CPGs developers have evidence-based knowledge superior to that of clinicians. Hoyt (1997, p. 32) states that the purpose of CPGs is to achieve: "reduction in unnecessary variability of care." Indeed, a prominent argument for adherence to CPGs has been to reduce "unnecessary" or "unwarranted" variation in clinical practice.

Wennberg (2011, p. 687) defines "unwarranted variation" as variation that: "isn't explained by illness or patient preference." The UK National Health Service gives its *Atlas of Variation in Healthcare* (2015) the subtitle "Reducing unwarranted variation to increase value and improve quality." Institute of Medicine states (2011, p. 26): "Trustworthy CPGs have the potential to reduce inappropriate practice variation." Another IOM report (2013) states:

geographic variation in spending is considered inappropriate or "unacceptable" when it is caused by or results in ineffective use of treatments, as by provider failure to adhere to established clinical practice guidelines. (pp. 2–15)

These and many similar quotations exemplify a widespread belief that adherence to guidelines is socially preferable to decentralized clinical decision making. Yet there has been an absence of welfare analysis to support this belief. Moreover, there has been a lack of consensus about how to distinguish warranted from unwarranted variation in patient care (Mercuri and Gafni, 2011).

There are at least two broad reasons why patient care adhering to guidelines may differ from the care that clinicians provide. First, guideline developers and clinicians may differ in their ability to predict how decisions affect patient outcomes. Second, guideline developers and clinicians may differ in how they evaluate patient outcomes. Welfare comparison of adherence to guidelines and decentralized decision making requires consideration of both factors, and perhaps others as well.

This book addresses how limited ability to assess patient risk of illness and to predict treatment response may affect the welfare achieved by adherence to guidelines and by decentralized clinical practice. Differences in evaluation of patient outcomes may be important as well. Institute of Medicine (2011) devotes considerable attention to the possibility that guideline developers may have financial or intellectual stakes that create conflicts between their personal interests and those of patients.

VARIATION IN GUIDELINES

Commentaries exhorting adherence to guidelines implicitly assume that guideline developers agree on appropriate patient care. Consensus holds in some cases, but the guidelines issued by distinct health organizations often differ from one another. Variation in care is inevitable if clinicians adhere to different guidelines.

A notable instance concerns performance of a clinical breast examination (CBE) in breast cancer screening. The guidelines issued by the National Comprehensive Cancer Network (NCCN), the American Cancer Society (ACS), and the US Preventive Services Task Force (USPSTF) differ markedly. The NCCN considers the CBE to be a core element of breast cancer screening, stating (2017, p. 40):

> The starting point of these guidelines for screening and evaluating breast abnormalities is a clinical encounter, which includes a complete medical history followed by breast cancer risk assessment and a CBE. . . . CBE is an important component of a clinical encounter and is important in order to detect early-stage palpable cancers.

The ACS takes a firmly negative position, stating (Oeffinger et al., 2015, p. 1608): "The ACS does not recommend clinical breast examination (CBE) for breast cancer screening among average-risk women at any age." The USPSTF is neutral, stating (2009, p. 716): "The USPSTF concludes that the current evidence is insufficient to assess the additional benefits and harms of clinical breast examination beyond screening mammography in women 40 years or older."

Some have argued that the existing variation in guidelines across health organizations stems in part from variation in the processes used to develop guidelines. Guyatt et al. (2008, p. 924) write: "Guideline developers around the world are inconsistent in how they rate quality of evidence and grade strength of recommendations." In an article focusing on guidelines commissioned by the World Health Organization (WHO), Schünemann et al. (2007) write:

> Clinical practice guidelines generally, and some WHO guidelines specifically, have been criticized for not being based on the best available evidence, for being exposed to undue influence by industry and experts who participate in guideline panels, and for not adhering to guidelines for preparing guidelines. Guidance that is not informed by the best available evidence or by statements that the available evidence is of low quality can harm patients, waste limited resources, and hinder research to address important uncertainties. (p. 786)

The authors thus carry the concern about unwarranted variation in clinical practice to a second level. They assert not only that clinicians should adhere to CPGs but that guideline developers should adhere to "guidelines for preparing guidelines."

A prominent set of guidelines for preparing guidelines is the GRADE system (Grading of Recommendations Assessment, Development and Evaluation) described in Guyatt et al. (2008). GRADE is a set of procedures for rating quality of evidence and strength of recommendations that has been promoted as having advantages over previous ratings systems. I will discuss and critique the GRADE procedures in chapter 4.

CASE STUDY: NODAL OBSERVATION OR DISSECTION IN TREATMENT OF MELANOMA

To illustrate variation in guidelines, I present a case study of choice between surveillance and aggressive treatment. The decision discussed is choice between *nodal observation* and *lymph node dissection* (aka *lymphadenectomy*) when treating early-stage melanoma patients at risk of metastasis. Nodal observation is non-invasive surveillance of lymph nodes by palpation and/or ultrasound scan. The National Cancer Institute (2018) defines lymph node dissection as "a surgical procedure in which the lymph nodes are removed and a sample of tissue is checked under a microscope for signs of cancer." Being invasive and having multiple possible side effects, dissection is commonly viewed as an aggressive treatment relative to nodal observation.

Choice between nodal observation and lymph node dissection may not be well known to the public at large, but it is a common decision that arises in early treatment of melanoma, breast cancer, and other forms of localized cancer. I focus on melanoma because there has long been controversy about the merits of dissection relative to observation in this context. Guidelines have evolved as information has accumulated, but the guidelines issued by distinct health organizations continue to differ today.

Before moving ahead, I reiterate the caution stated in the introduction. Having no formal training in medicine, I refrain from dispensing medical advice regarding specific aspects of patient care. I do my best to communicate accurately the objectives and findings of medical research. With this in mind, I often quote the medical literature verbatim below. This should help to separate what authors have intended from my interpretation of their statements.

The Incubator and Marker Hypotheses

The controversy has stemmed in part from uncertainty about the physiological process through which melanoma spreads within the body. Faries (2018), beginning an editorial on choice between nodal observation and lymph node dissection, commented on the history this way:

> For surgeons caring for patients with melanoma, treatment of regional lymph nodes has been controversial for well over a century. Over that time, two groups Galen might recognize as "sects" developed. One group, proponents of the "incubator" hypothesis, felt metastasis progresses sequentially, first to regional nodes and then on to distant sites. For them, early nodal surgery saves lives. The opposing "marker" hypothesis saw lymph nodes merely as indicators of a metastatic phenotype, with surgical intervention unable to alter outcomes. As data became available to test these rival proposals, it is interesting to note how often the same information has been used to support contradictory conclusions. (p. 1)

Faries's mention of "Galen" refers to the ancient Greek physician and philosopher of that name. He opens his editorial by citing Galen's statement: "The fact is that those who are enslaved to their sects are not merely devoid of all sound knowledge, but they will not even stop to learn!"

The incubator and marker hypotheses propose different theories of how a primary melanoma—a tumor that develops de novo at a specific location—spreads to distant parts of the body. The incubator hypothesis asserts that malignant cells first travel from the primary melanoma through the lymphatic system to a regional lymph node basin near the primary location. Metastasis in these lymph nodes becomes an "incubator" that enables malignant cells to travel onward from affected nodes to internal organs. Under this hypothesis, lymph node dissection may have therapeutic value, preventing malignant cells from reaching internal organs. This therapeutic value, if present, may be important because melanoma in internal organs generates a high rate of fatality.

The marker hypothesis asserts that malignant cells may travel from the primary melanoma to internal organs through routes other than the regional lymph nodes, particularly through the bloodstream. Under this hypothesis, lymph node dissection does not prevent spread of the disease. A finding of malignant cells in the regional lymph nodes is only a "marker" of disease spread.

The marker hypothesis dismisses the possibility that dissection has therapeutic value, but it retains the possibility that dissection has informational value as a diagnostic test. Microscopic detection of malignant cells in the lymph nodes, not apparent in clinical observation of the nodes, may suggest that the patient has high risk of metastasis elsewhere. Oncologists often summarize the informational value of dissection by saying that it may be useful for "staging" melanoma, where "stage" refers to a prevalent ordinal measure of severity of the disease.

The incubator and marker hypotheses conjecture two possibilities. If the incubator hypothesis describes reality, there may be good reason to prefer dissection to nodal observation. Prevention of spread of melanoma to internal organs, which is very often fatal, may be a major health benefit relative to observation. The possible side effects of dissection, which range from immediate surgical complications to lymphedema later, are non-trivial but generally are not fatal.

If the marker hypothesis describes reality, there may be good reason to prefer nodal observation to dissection. In this case, the possible benefits of dissection are limited to prevention of recurrence of disease in the lymph nodes and provision of information useful in staging. The possible side effects of dissection remain unchanged.

The degree to which either hypothesis describes reality remains unsettled today. Modern researchers appear to agree that melanoma may in principle spread either through the lymphatic system or the bloodstream, but they don't agree on the prevalence or determinants of each route. Leiter et al. (2016, p. 757) write: "In two-thirds of patients with melanoma, metastasis mainly develops in the regional lymph node basin, whereas in a third of patients, direct development of distant metastases has been observed." Gassenmaier et al. (2017) report that, within the highly selected subpopulation of patients with stage IV melanoma whom they study, the disease spread only through the lymphatic system in 38 percent of cases, through both the lymphatic system and the bloodstream in 45 percent, and only through the bloodstream in 16 percent.

Kasumova, Haynes, and Boland (2017) argue that the route of disease spread is affected by patient-specific biological heterogeneity across tumors. They seek to reorient the thinking of oncologists away from any unitary theory of spread, writing:

> Rather than refuting or supporting a specific hypothesis of metastasis, the field of melanoma oncology should focus on underlying tumor and immune-based biology that correlates with differences in metastatic patterns and the timing/location of failures. (p. 2468)

Reasonable Care Today

Complement 1A overviews the history of research on lymph node dissection, focusing on the important developments following the introduction of sentinel lymph node (SLN) biopsy in the 1990s. The advent of SLN biopsy, a much less invasive diagnostic test, has led to a clear consensus today that lymph node dissection should not be a routine procedure recommended for patients with early-stage melanoma. In the United States and some other countries, it has become a standard practice to perform SLN biopsy when the primary melanoma has intermediate thickness or greater. However, it remains an open question whether dissection should be performed when SLN biopsy shows microscopic evidence of malignancy in a sentinel node.

A case vignette in the *New England Journal of Medicine* recognizes that choice between nodal observation and dissection following detection of malignancy in a sentinel node remains an open question (Caulley et al., 2018). The vignette describes a patient in this setting, presents opposing recommendations posed by different clinicians, and invites readers to contribute their own views online. The journal introduces this intriguing way to stimulate discussion among clinicians:

> This interactive feature addresses the approach to a clinical issue. A case vignette is followed by specific options, neither of which can be considered either correct or incorrect. In short essays, experts in the field

then argue for each of the options. Readers can participate in forming community opinion by choosing one of the options and, if they like, providing their reasons. (p. 85)

The question being open, it should not be surprising to find variation in care today. Complement 1A documents that guidelines vary between British and American health organizations. This variation should not necessarily be interpreted as unnecessary or unwarranted. It may rather reflect uncertainty about the relative merits of nodal observation and dissection, combined with variation in the decision criteria that clinicians and patients use in the presence of this uncertainty. As I will discuss in chapter 6, variation in care may be useful from a population-health perspective, yielding some of the error-limitation and learning benefits of diversification.

One ordinarily thinks that uncertainty about the outcomes of patient care decisions should diminish over time, as new research accumulates. Yet new research sometimes increases uncertainty, at least for a while. Assessment of nodal observation and dissection may be such a case, a consequence of research yielding new immunotherapy treatments for melanoma.

The currently available evidence on survival outcomes with nodal observation or dissection was obtained in an environment that lacked effective systemic treatments for melanoma that spreads to internal organs. McGregor (2013) mentions this in her critique of SLN biopsy, writing that the procedure: "does not direct further management in melanoma because we have no effective adjuvant intervention as yet" (pp. 233–234).

The prospects for adjuvant intervention have improved recently with the development of new immunotherapies targeted for patients with specific characteristics. See Eggermont and Dummer (2017) for a review. These treatment innovations offer new hope to patients, but they may reduce the usefulness of the evidence obtained in research performed prior to discovery of the new immunotherapies.

Use of historical data on treatment response to inform future treatment choice generally rests on the assumption that future patients will respond as did past ones. Extrapolation from the past to the future is credible in a stable environment, but it may be wishful otherwise. It seems reasonable to expect that introduction of effective systemic treatments for melanoma will improve patient survival prospects with both nodal observation and dissection. It may be more difficult to predict how the new systemic treatments will affect survival prospects with nodal observation relative to those with dissection.

1.2. Degrees of Personalized Medicine

The term *personalized medicine* is sometimes defined to mean health care that is literally specific to the individual, as in this definition by Ginsburg and Willard (2009, p. 278): "Personalized medicine is . . . health care that is informed by each person's unique clinical, genetic, genomic, and environmental information." Yet evidence to support complete personalization is rarely available. Hence, the term is commonly used to mean care that varies with some individual characteristics. With the same idea in mind, clinicians may refer to *stratified* or *precision* medicine.

President's Council of Advisors on Science and Technology (2008, p. 7) states:

> "Personalized medicine" refers to the tailoring of medical treatment to the specific characteristics of each patient. In an operational sense, however, personalized medicine does not literally mean the creation of drugs or medical devices that are unique to a patient. Rather, it involves the ability to classify individuals into subpopulations that are uniquely or disproportionately susceptible to a particular disease or responsive to a specific treatment.

Academy of Medical Sciences (2015, p. 4) states:

> The terms "stratified," "personalised" or "precision" medicine all refer to the grouping of patients based on risk of disease, or response to therapy, using diagnostic tests or techniques.

Thus, personalized medicine is a matter of degree rather than an all-or-nothing proposition.

Clinicians classify patients into groups based on observed medical history and the results of screening and diagnostic tests. Clinical practice guidelines recommend classifications that aim to be well-grounded in evidence on risk of disease and treatment response. The classification rules used depend on the available evidence on group outcomes.

Personalized probabilities of disease development or treatment outcomes depend on the patient attributes used to condition the predictions. Clinicians often observe patient attributes beyond those used to predict outcomes in evidence-based risk assessments and studies of treatment response. Hence, clinicians often can personalize patient care to a greater degree than do evidence-based CPGs.

PREDICTION OF CARDIOVASCULAR DISEASE

An apt illustration of how available evidence affects risk assessment is the ASCVD Risk Estimator of the American College of Cardiology (2017), which predicts the probability that a person will develop atherosclerotic cardiovascular disease (ASCVD) in the next ten years. This online tool conditions the reported probability on these attributes:

Patient Demographics: current age, sex, race (white/African American/other).

Current Labs/Exams: total cholesterol, HDL cholesterol, LDL cholesterol, systolic blood pressure.

Personal History: history of diabetes (yes/no), on hypertension treatment (yes/no), smoker (yes, former, no), on a statin (yes/no), on aspirin therapy (yes/no).

The predictions of the ASCVD Risk Estimator are based on the Pooled Cohort Equations described by Karmali et al. (2014) and on the findings of other studies. The ASCVD Risk Estimator personalizes predicted risk in many respects, but it does not make predictions using further observable patient attributes that may be associated with risk of ASCVD. For example, it does not condition the prediction on patient obesity, job stress, and exercise.

THE BREAST CANCER RISK ASSESSMENT TOOL

Another apt illustration is the Breast Cancer Risk Assessment (BCRA) Tool of the National Cancer Institute (2011). The BCRA Tool gives an evidence-based probability that a woman will develop breast cancer conditional on eight attributes:

(1) history of breast cancer or chest radiation therapy for Hodgkin's Lymphoma (yes/no).

(2) presence of a BRCA mutation or diagnosis of a genetic syndrome associated with risk of breast cancer (yes/no/unknown).

(3) current age, in years.

(4) age of first menstrual period (7–11, 12–13, ≥ 14, unknown).

(5) age of first live birth of a child (no births, < 20, 20–24, 25–29, ≥ 30, unknown).

(6) number of first-degree female relatives with breast cancer (0, 1, >1, unknown).

(7) number of breast biopsies (0, 1, > 1, unknown).
(8) race/ethnicity (white, African American, Hispanic, Asian American, American Indian or Alaskan Native, unknown).

The BCRA Tool has become widely used in clinical practice (Susan G. Komen, 2016) and is an important input to the CPG for breast cancer screening issued by the National Comprehensive Cancer Network (2017).

The reason that the BCRA Tool assesses risk conditional on these eight attributes and not others is that it uses a modified version of the "Gail Model," based on the empirical research of Gail et al. (1989). The Gail et al. article estimated probabilities of breast cancer for white women who have annual breast examinations, conditional on attributes (1) through (7). Scientists at the National Cancer Institute later modified the model to predict invasive cancer within a wider population of women.

The BCRA Tool personalizes predicted risk of breast cancer in many respects, but it does not condition on further observable patient attributes that may be associated with risk of cancer. When considering the number of first-degree relatives with breast cancer (attribute 6), the Tool does not consider the number and ages of a woman's first-degree relatives, nor the ages when any of them developed breast cancer. These factors should be informative when interpreting the response to the item. Nor does it condition on the prevalence of breast cancer among second-degree relatives, a consideration that figures in another risk assessment model due to Claus, Risch, and Thompson (1994). When considering race/ethnicity (attribute 8), the BCRA Tool groups all white women together and does not distinguish subgroups such as Ashkenazi Jews, who are thought to have considerably higher risk of a BRCA mutation than other white subgroups, a potentially important matter when the answer regarding attribute (2) is "unknown." Moreover, the BCRA Tool does not condition on behavioral attributes such as excessive drinking of alcohol, which has been associated with increased risk of breast cancer (Singletary and Gapstur, 2001).

PREDICTING UNREALISTICALLY PRECISE PROBABILITIES

A user of the ASCVD Risk Estimator or the BCRA Tool who inputs the required personal attributes receives in response a precise probability of disease development. Yet statistical imprecision and identification problems make these risk assessments uncertain. Recall that statistical imprecision is the problem of drawing inferences about a study population by observing a finite sample of its members. Identification problems are inferential difficulties such as missing data that persist even when sample size grows without bound.

Without discussion of uncertainty, clinicians and patients may mistakenly believe that precise probabilistic risk assessments are accurate. If uncertainty is not quantified, those who recognize the presence of uncertainty cannot evaluate the degree to which assessments may be inaccurate. I call attention here to the existence of statistical imprecision in the predictions, focusing on the BCRA Tool. Later chapters will discuss multiple identification problems.

As mentioned above, the BCRA Tool implements a modified form of the Gail Model introduced in the research article of Gail et al. (1989). The article is careful to call attention to statistical imprecision in its estimates of the probability of developing cancer over various future age intervals. It describes a general procedure for estimating confidence intervals for its risk assessments. It reports illustrative computations of 95% confidence intervals for two women with different specified attributes.

The computed confidence intervals, presented in table 5 of the article, are revealing. They vary considerably in width, indicating that statistical imprecision is much more an issue when assessing risks for some women than for others. Consider, for example, the Gail et al. predictions of the percentage chance that a woman will develop breast cancer during the age interval 40–70 years. For Subject 1, the estimated percentage chance is 10.1 and the confidence interval for this estimate is [8.4, 12.2], an interval of width 3.8. For Subject 2, the estimated percentage chance is 39.8 and the confidence interval for this estimate is [25.1, 60.5], an interval of width 35.4. Thus, a clinician might reasonably ignore statistical imprecision when using the Gail Model to assess risk for Subject 1, but the clinician should be aware that there is considerable imprecision when using the model to assess risk for Subject 2.

While the Gail et al. article is forthright in its evaluation of statistical imprecision, the BCRA Tool that implements a version of the Gail Model does not report confidence intervals. Indeed, the NCI website that houses the BCRA Tool makes no mention of statistical imprecision. If a clinician were to input the attributes of Subjects 1 and 2, the Tool would output a precise risk assessment for each one, without even a verbal caution that the assessment for Subject 2 is much less precise than that for Subject 1.

1.3. Optimal Care Assuming Rational Expectations

The BCRA Tool and the ASCVD Risk Estimator exemplify a common question in patient care. Evidence from medical research enables assessment of risk of disease or treatment response conditional on certain patient attributes, so guidelines make recommendations conditional on these attributes. Clinicians observe additional attributes that may be informative predictors of patient outcomes, but the available evidence does not show how outcomes vary with the additional attributes. How should medical decision making proceed?

Economists have studied this question in an idealized setting of individualistic patient care with rational expectations. This setting supposes that a clinician must choose how to treat each person in a population of patients. The clinician observes certain attributes for each patient. The objective is to maximize a social welfare function that sums up the benefits and costs of treatment across the population of patients.

It is usually assumed that the clinician views benefits and costs from the perspective of each patient and aims to do what is best for the patient. Pauly (1980) refers to a clinician acting in this manner as an "agent" for the patient. In economics jargon, the clinician is assumed to be *utilitarian*, a term dating to Jeremy Bentham in the late 1700s. A utilitarian welfare function formalizes the familiar idea of patient-centered care. The assumption of individualistic care means that the care received by one patient may affect that person but does not affect other members of the population. This assumption is usually realistic when considering non-infectious diseases. I assume throughout this book that care is individualistic.

A central idealization of the setting studied by economists is to assume that the clinician knows the actual probability distribution of health outcomes that may potentially occur if a patient with specified observed attributes is given a specified treatment. As a shorthand, economists say that the clinician has *rational expectations*, a term that originated in macroeconomics in the 1960s. The assumption of rational expectations does not go so far as to assert that the clinician can predict patient outcomes with certainty—that assumption is called *perfect foresight*. Rational expectations means that the clinician makes accurate probabilistic predictions conditional on observed patient attributes. I say that the assumption of rational expectations is an idealization because we shall later find considerable basis to question its realism.

If a clinician has rational expectations, the problem of optimizing patient care has a simple solution. Patients should be divided into groups that have the same observed attributes. All patients in an attribute group should be given the care that yields the highest within-group mean welfare. Thus, it is optimal to differentially treat patients with different observed attributes if different treatments maximize their within-group mean welfare. Patients with the same observed attributes should be treated uniformly. The value of maximum welfare increases as more patient attributes are observed.

These findings have long been known and are often stated without attribution. I do not know who first proved them, but a relatively early abstract version is given by Good (1967). The results have been proved and used in the economic literature on medical decision making by Phelps and Mushlin (1988), Meltzer (2001), Basu and Meltzer (2007), and Manski (2013b), among others.

OPTIMAL CHOICE BETWEEN SURVEILLANCE AND AGGRESSIVE TREATMENT

Consider choice between surveillance and aggressive treatment of patients at risk of potential disease. As discussed in the introduction, this decision often requires resolution of a tension between benefits and costs. Aggressive treatment may be more beneficial to the extent that it reduces the risk of disease development or the severity of disease that does develop. However, it may be more harmful to the extent that it generates health side effects and financial costs beyond those associated with surveillance.

Complement 1B formally considers a simple but instructive version of the decision problem. I view it as a one-time choice rather than a dynamic decision that can be revisited and updated over time. I show that the optimization problem is particularly simple when aggressive treatment affects disease in one of two polar ways. In one polar case, aggressive treatment prevents the occurrence of disease. In the other, it does not affect the occurrence of disease, but it reduces the severity of disease when it occurs.

In these settings I find that aggressive treatment is the better option if the probability of disease development exceeds a computable patient-specific threshold. Surveillance is the better option otherwise.

1.4. Psychological Research Comparing Evidence-Based Prediction and Clinical Judgment

If clinicians have rational expectations, there is no utilitarian argument to develop and publish CPGs. However, a body of research in psychology has concluded that evidence-based predictions made with assessment tools consistently outperform ones made by clinical judgment when the predictions are made using the same patient attributes. The gap in performance persists even when clinical judgment uses additional attributes as predictors.

This research began in the mid-twentieth century, notable early contributions including Sarbin (1943, 1944), Meehl (1954), and Goldberg (1968). To describe the conclusions of the literature, I rely mainly on the review article of Dawes, Faust, and Meehl (1989). See Camerer and Johnson (1997) and Groves et al. (2000) for further review articles.

Dawes et al. (1989) distinguish evidence-based (or actuarial or statistical) prediction and clinical judgment as follows:

> In the clinical method the decision-maker combines or processes information in his or her head. In the actuarial or statistical method the human judge is eliminated and conclusions rest solely on empirically established relations between data and the condition or event of interest. (p. 1668)

Comparing the two in circumstances where a clinician observes patient attributes that are not utilized in available evidence-based prediction, they state:

> Might the clinician attain superiority if given an informational edge? For example, suppose the clinician lacks an actuarial formula for interpreting certain interview results and must choose between an impression based on both interview and test scores and a contrary actuarial interpretation based on only the test scores. The research addressing this question has yielded consistent results. . . . Even when given an information edge, the clinical judge still fails to surpass the actuarial method; in fact, access to additional information often does nothing to close the gap between the two methods. (p. 1670)

Seeking to explain this empirical finding, Dawes et al. (1989) discuss an example in which the additional observed attribute is that a patient has a broken leg and then write:

> The broken leg possibility is easily studied by providing clinicians with both the available data and the actuarial conclusion and allowing them to use or countervail the latter at their discretion. The limited research examining this possibility, however, all shows that greater overall accuracy is achieved when clinicians rely uniformly on actuarial conclusions and avoid discretionary judgments. . . . When operating freely, clinicians

apparently identify too many "exceptions," that is, the actuarial conclusions correctly modified are outnumbered by those incorrectly modified. If clinicians were more conservative in overriding actuarial conclusions they might gain an advantage, but this conjecture remains to be studied adequately. (pp. 1670–1671)

Here and elsewhere, Dawes, Faust, and Meehl caution against use of clinical judgment to subjectively predict disease risk or treatment response conditional on patient attributes that are not utilized in evidence-based predictors. They attribute the weak performance of clinical judgment to clinician failure to adequately grasp the logic of the prediction problem and to their use of decision rules that place too much emphasis on exceptions such as broken legs.

Psychological research published after Dawes et al. (1989) has largely corroborated the conclusions reached there, albeit occasionally with caveats. For example, Groves et al. (2000) conclude their review of the literature as follows:

This study confirms and greatly extends previous reports that mechanical prediction is typically as accurate or more accurate than clinical prediction. However, our results qualify overbroad statements in the literature opining that such superiority is completely uniform; it is not. In half of the studies we analyzed, the clinical method is approximately as good as mechanical prediction, and in a few scattered instances, the clinical method was notably more accurate. (p. 25)

Even though outlier studies can be found, we identified no systematic exceptions to the general superiority (or at least material equivalence) of mechanical prediction. It holds in general medicine, in mental health, in personality, and in education and training settings. It holds for medically trained judges and for psychologists. It holds for inexperienced and seasoned judges.

It is natural to ask how psychological research on clinical judgment has affected the practice of medicine. Curiously, I have found no explicit reference to it in my reading of medical commentaries advocating adherence to CPGs, nor in the broader literature concerning practice of evidence-based medicine. I have found passages in the literature on evidence-based medicine that, contrary to the psychological literature, praise rather than criticize clinical judgment. For example, Sackett (1997) calls for integration of evidence-based research and clinical judgment, writing:

The practice of evidence-based medicine means integrating individual clinical expertise with the best available external clinical evidence from systematic research. By individual clinical expertise we mean the proficiency and judgment that we individual clinicians acquire through clinical experience and clinical practice. . . . By best available external clinical evidence we mean clinically relevant research. . . . Good doctors use both individual clinical expertise and the best available external evidence, and neither alone is enough. (p. 3)

Similarly, the authors of an article reporting an evidence-based CPG for management of high blood pressure (James et al., 2014, p. 507) write:

Although this guideline provides evidence-based recommendations for the management of high BP and should meet the clinical needs of most patients, these recommendations are not a substitute for clinical judgment, and decisions about care must carefully consider and incorporate the clinical characteristics and circumstances of each individual patient.

1.5. Second-Best Welfare Comparison of Adherence to Guidelines and Clinical Judgment

The psychological literature challenges the realism of assuming that clinicians have rational expectations. However, this literature does not per se imply that adherence to CPGs would yield greater welfare than decentralized decision making using clinical judgment. For specificity, I will again consider choice between surveillance and aggressive treatment.

One issue is that the psychological literature has not addressed all welfare-relevant aspects of clinical decisions. Optimal decisions are determined by disease probabilities and by patient preferences regarding health outcomes. For example, some patients may be mainly concerned about their life spans while others may put considerable weight on quality of life. Psychologists have studied the relative accuracy of risk assessments and diagnoses made by evidence-based predictors and by clinicians. However, they have not similarly studied the relative accuracy of evaluations of patient preferences. Thus, the literature has generated findings that may be informative about the accuracy of risk assessments but not about patient preferences.

A second issue is that psychological research has seldom examined the accuracy of probabilistic risk assessments and diagnoses. It has been more common to assess the accuracy of point predictions. However, study of the logical relationship between probabilistic and point prediction shows that data on the latter at most yield wide bounds on the former. Manski (1990a) considers a forecaster who is asked to translate a probabilistic risk assessment into a yes/no point prediction that a patient will develop a potential disease. With reasonable assumptions about the translation process, observation that the forecaster states "yes" or "no" only implies that he judges the probability to be in the interval [½, 1] or [0, ½], respectively. Thus, analysis of the accuracy of point predictions does not reveal much about the accuracy of evidence-based and clinical assessment of disease probabilities.

Given these issues, it is not possible at present to conclude that imperfect clinical judgment makes adherence to CPGs superior to decentralized decision making. The findings of the psychological literature only imply that welfare comparison is a delicate matter of choice between alternative second-best systems for patient care. Adherence to evidence-based CPGs may be inferior to the extent that CPGs condition on fewer patient attributes than do clinicians, but it may be superior to the extent that imperfect clinical judgment yields suboptimal decisions. How these opposing forces interplay depends on the specifics of the setting.

SURVEILLANCE OR AGGRESSIVE TREATMENT OF WOMEN AT RISK OF BREAST CANCER

To illustrate, consider the common clinical decision between surveillance and aggressive treatment of women at risk of breast cancer. In this setting, surveillance usually means that a woman receives a breast examination and mammogram periodically, annually or biannually depending on age. Aggressive treatment encompasses several options.

One is more frequent surveillance. This does not affect the risk of disease development, but it may reduce the severity of disease outcomes by enabling earlier diagnosis and treatment of the tumor. A potential side effect, whose severity is uncertain, may be an increased risk of cancer caused by the radiation from mammograms.

Other options for aggressive treatment include strategies for reduction of the risk of disease development. These include changes to diet, administration of a drug such as tamoxifen, and preventive mastectomy. Each strategy may have side effects, most obviously in the case of preventive mastectomy.

Analysis of optimal care with rational expectations suggests that, ceteris paribus, some form of aggressive treatment is the better option if the risk of breast cancer is sufficiently high and that surveillance is better otherwise. Some CPGs use the BCRA Tool to assess risk and recommend aggressive treatment if the predicted probability of invasive cancer in the next five years is above a specified threshold. National Comprehensive Cancer Network (2017) recommends annual surveillance if the predicted probability is below 0.017 and choice of some form of aggressive treatment if the probability is higher. A guideline issued by the American Society of Clinical Oncology (ASCO) recommends consideration of a pharmacological intervention when the predicted probability is above 0.0166 (Visvanathan et al., 2009).

A clinician could use judgment to assess risk conditional on a richer set of patient attributes than are used in the BCRA Tool. He could also use a personalized threshold probability to choose treatment, rather than apply the value 0.017 or 0.0166 to all patients. However, clinical judgment may be imperfect. As far as I am aware, it is not known whether adherence to the NCCN or ASCO guideline yields better or worse outcomes than does decentralized clinical decision making.

2

Wishful Extrapolation from Research to Patient Care

The psychological literature discussed in chapter 1 has questioned the judgment of clinicians, but it has not similarly questioned the accuracy of the predictions used in evidence-based guideline development. The fact that predictions are evidence-based does not ensure that they use the available evidence effectively. Multiple questionable methodological practices have long afflicted research on health outcomes and the development of guidelines.

This chapter mainly focuses on predictions using evidence from randomized trials. Trials have long enjoyed a favored status within medical research on treatment response and are often called the "gold standard" for such research. The US Food and Drug Administration (FDA) ordinarily considers only trial data when making decisions on drug approval (Fisher and Moyé, 1999).

The influential *Cochrane Handbook for Systematic Reviews of Interventions* (Higgins and Green, 2011, sec. 5.5) views trials as qualitatively superior to observational studies, writing:

> Because Cochrane reviews address questions about the effects of health care, they focus primarily on randomized trials. Randomization is the only way to prevent systematic differences between baseline characteristics of participants in different intervention groups in terms of both known and unknown (or unmeasured) confounders. . . . For clinical

interventions, deciding who receives an intervention and who does not is influenced by many factors, including prognostic factors. Empirical evidence suggests that, on average, non-randomized studies produce effect estimates that indicate more extreme benefits of the effects of health care than randomized trials. However, the extent, and even the direction, of the bias is difficult to predict.

The *Cochrane Handbook* goes on to discuss the GRADE approach to rating the certainty of a body of evidence, the four rating levels being (high, moderate, low, very low). GRADE recommends that the "high" rating should be reserved for evidence from certain randomized trials. The Cochrane authors write (sec. 12.2.1): "Review authors will generally grade evidence from sound observational studies as low quality."

Guideline developers act accordingly, valuing trial evidence more than observational studies. Indeed, guideline developers sometimes choose to use only trial evidence, excluding observational studies from consideration. An example is the James et al. (2014) article reporting a new CPG for management of high blood pressure. The authors write: "The panel limited its evidence review to RCTs because they are less subject to bias than other study designs and represent the gold standard for determining efficacy and effectiveness" (p. 508).

The well-known appeal of trials is that, given sufficient sample size and complete observation of outcomes, they deliver credible findings about treatment response within the study population. However, it is also well-known that extrapolation of findings from trials to clinical practice can be difficult. Researchers and guideline developers often use untenable assumptions to extrapolate. I have referred to this practice as *wishful extrapolation* (Manski, 2013a).

This chapter discusses multiple reasons why extrapolation of research findings to clinical practice may be suspect. Chapter 3 will deepen the discussion of use of evidence to inform patient care, considering both trial data and observational studies.

2.1. From Study Populations to Patient Populations

The study populations in trials often differ from the patient populations that clinicians treat. Trial designs often mandate important differences between these populations. A common practice has been to perform trials concerned with treatment of a specific disease only on subjects who have no comorbidities or who have specific comorbidities. Patients treated in practice may suffer from multiple conditions. Clinicians may then need to choose complexes of interacting treatments rather than treat diseases in isolation from one another.

Guideline developers sometimes caution about the difficulty of using trial findings to make care recommendations for patients with comorbidities. The problem is well-stated by Wong et al. (2017) in an article presenting updated guidelines for treatment of melanoma. The guideline panel wrote:

> Creating evidence-based recommendations to inform treatment of patients with additional chronic conditions, a situation in which the patient may have two or more such conditions—referred to as multiple chronic conditions (MCC)—is challenging. Patients with MCC are a complex and heterogeneous population, making it difficult to account for all the possible permutations to develop specific recommendations for care. In addition, the best available evidence for treating index conditions, such as cancer, is often from clinical trials whose study selection criteria may exclude these patients to avoid potential interaction effects or confounding of results associated with MCC. As a result, the reliability of outcome data from these studies may be limited, thereby creating constraints for expert groups to make recommendations for care in this heterogeneous patient population. (pp. 13–14)

Another source of difference between study and clinical populations is that a study population consists of persons with stipulated demographic attributes who volunteer to participate in a trial. Participation in a trial may be restricted to persons in certain age categories who reside in certain locales. Among such persons, volunteers are those who respond to financial and medical incentives to participate. A financial incentive may be receipt of free treatments. A medical incentive is that participation in a trial opens the possibility of receiving a treatment that is not otherwise available.

The study population differs materially from the relevant patient population if subjects and non-subjects have different distributions of treatment response. Treatment response in the latter group is not observed. It may be wishful extrapolation to assume that treatment response observed in trials performed on volunteers with stipulated demographic attributes who lack comorbidities is the same as what would occur in actual patient populations.

A practical problem facing clinicians who wish to assess the closeness of study populations to patient populations is that the journal articles reporting trial findings often describe the compositions of their study populations incompletely. Blümle et al. (2011) studied this matter in one research setting and concluded as follows:

> We showed that the eligibility criteria published in trial reports do not adequately reflect those prespecified in the study protocols. This may have consequences for clinical practice, research, and policy. Even if a reader has precise information about a trial's study population, the interpretation of published results of therapeutic research is fraught with problems. In contrast with a study's internal validity, its applicability cannot be assessed without substantial information that goes beyond the study itself. Often it is unclear whether an experimental intervention is also effective in a different clinical scenario. The difficulties in using trial results in clinical practice, research, and policy augment if the published information on the study populations is incomplete or reported selectively. (p. 6)

TRIALS OF DRUG TREATMENTS FOR HYPERTENSION

Trials of drug treatments for hypertension illustrate how study populations may differ from patient populations. Numerous such trials have been performed on a wide variety of study populations. Evidence from dozens of trials was utilized by the Eighth Joint National Committee (JNC 8), which promulgated the 2014 guidelines for management of high blood pressure in the United States (James et al., 2014).

The JNC 8 highlighted three trials, described in Beckett et al. (2008), SHEP Cooperative Research Group (1991), and Staessen et al. (1997). It is instructive to juxtapose the study populations of these trials. The participants differed in age, in countries of residence, and in the rules governing exclusions for comorbidities. Moreover, they differed in their blood pressure levels measured at two stages before being randomized into treatment. The SHEP and Staessen trials, but not the Beckett trial, restricted eligibility to persons diagnosed as having *isolated systolic hypertension*, a condition in which systolic blood pressure is higher than desirable but diastolic blood pressure is in the normal range. I provide some details of the study populations below, drawing on descriptions in the published articles.

Beckett trial: Participants were eighty years of age or older, residing in Europe, China, Australasia, and Tunisia. Persons with various comorbidities were excluded. To be eligible, a person initially had to have a sustained systolic blood pressure of 160 mmHg or more. This group included persons who were and were not receiving antihypertensive treatment at the time. Persons with blood pressure in the eligible initial range consented to stop treatment for several months, after which they were required to have systolic blood pressure in the range 160–199 mmHg and diastolic blood pressure below 110 mmHg. Persons in this subgroup were randomized to a drug treatment or to placebo.

SHEP trial: Participants were sixty years of age or older, residing in the United States. Persons with various comorbidities were excluded. To be eligible, a person initially had to have a systolic blood pressure in a certain range, the specifics depending on whether they were or were not receiving antihypertensive treatment at the time. Persons with blood pressure in the eligible initial range consented to stop treatment for several months, after which they were required to have systolic blood pressure in the range 160–219 mmHg and diastolic blood pressure below 90 mmHg. Persons in this subgroup were randomized to a drug treatment or to placebo.

Staessen trial: Participants were sixty years of age or older, residing in Europe. Persons with various comorbidities were excluded. The published article does not state whether a person initially had to have a systolic blood pressure in some range. Potential subjects consented to stop treatment for several months, after which they were required to have systolic blood pressure in the range 160–219 mmHg and diastolic blood pressure below 95 mmHg. Persons in this subgroup were randomized to a drug treatment or to placebo.

CAMPBELL AND THE PRIMACY OF INTERNAL VALIDITY

Seeking to justify analysis of trials performed on study populations that may differ substantially from the populations that clinicians treat, researchers in population health and the social sciences often cite Donald Campbell, who distinguished between the internal and external validity of studies of treatment response (Campbell and Stanley, 1963; Campbell, 1984). A study is said to have *internal validity* if its findings for the study population are credible. It has *external validity* if an invariance assumption permits credible extrapolation. In this terminology, the appeal of randomized trials is their internal validity. Wishful extrapolation is an absence of external validity.

Campbell argued that studies should be judged first by their internal validity and secondarily by their external validity. This perspective has been used to argue for the primacy of experimental research over observational studies, whatever the study population may be. The reason given is that properly executed randomized experiments have high internal validity. The Campbell perspective has also been used to argue that the best observational studies are those that most closely approximate randomized experiments.

Campbell's view has been endorsed by Rosenbaum (1999), who recommends that observational studies of human subjects aim to approximate the conditions of laboratory experiments. Rosenbaum, like Campbell, downplays the importance of having the study population be similar to the population of interest, writing: "Studies of samples that are representative of populations may be quite useful in describing those populations, but may be ill-suited to inferences about treatment effects" (p. 259).

From the perspective of treatment choice, the Campbell-Rosenbaum position is well grounded if treatment response is homogeneous. Then researchers can aim to learn about treatment response in easy-to-analyze study populations, and clinicians can be confident that research findings can be extrapolated to patient populations of interest. In human populations, however, homogeneity of treatment response may be the exception rather than the rule. To the degree that treatment response is heterogeneous, it may be wishful to extrapolate findings from a study population to a patient population of interest, as optimal treatments in the two may differ. Hence, I see no general reason to value internal validity above external validity.

2.2. From Experimental Treatments to Clinical Treatments

Treatments in trials often differ from those that would occur in clinical practice. I discuss two reasons that may create difficulties in extrapolating trial findings to patient care.

INTENSITY OF TREATMENT

Patients typically obtain more intensive attention in trials than in practice. They may receive more frequent diagnostic tests and more face-to-face contact with clinicians. Receiving more attention, patients may adhere more closely to clinical visit schedules and treatment regimens than they would in ordinary practice.

An example is use of warfarin as a treatment for patients with atrial fibrillation. Go et al. (2003) observed that participants in trials evaluating warfarin therapy are monitored more closely than they would be in practice and cautioned that this may be consequential. They wrote:

Multiple randomized trials have demonstrated warfarin therapy to be highly efficacious in reducing risk of ischemic stroke and other systemic thromboembolism in patients with atrial fibrillation, with relatively low rates of bleeding. . . . However, concerns persist about the effectiveness and safety of anticoagulation with warfarin in persons treated in usual clinical care because the randomized trials enrolled highly selected patients, included few very elderly patients, and closely monitored anticoagulation. This has important clinical implications because atrial fibrillation occurs commonly, particularly among the elderly, and because the potential benefits vs risks of warfarin therapy are dependent on good control of anticoagulation intensity. (p. 2685)

Concern with the credibility of extrapolating trial findings to clinical practice motivated the authors to perform an observational study to obtain relevant evidence.

Intensity of treatment in trials and in practice may also differ when treatment effectiveness depends on the skills of the clinicians administering them, as with surgery and psychological counseling. The clinicians who treat patients in trials may have different skills than those who treat patients in practice. Then extrapolation of trial findings to general patient care may be difficult.

BLINDING IN DRUG TRIALS

Trials comparing drug treatments are normally double-blinded, with neither the patient nor the clinician knowing the assigned treatment. Examples are the Becket, SHEP, and Staessen trials discussed above. A double-blinded drug trial reveals the distribution of response in a setting where the patient and clinician are uncertain what treatment the patient is receiving. It does not reveal what response would be in the usual clinical setting where the patient and clinician know what drug is being administered and can react to this information.

Consider drug treatments for hypertension. It is well-known that patients react heterogeneously to the various drugs that are available for prescription, some drugs working better for certain patients and others working better for other patients. Materson et al. (1993, p. 920) write: "Antihypertensive treatment must be tailored to the individual patient." Recognizing this, a clinician treating a patient may sequentially prescribe alternative drugs, trying each for a period of time in an effort to find one that performs satisfactorily.

Sequential experimentation is not possible in a trial, where the standard protocol prohibits the clinician from knowing what drug a subject is receiving and from using judgment to modify the treatment. Hence, the patient outcomes observed in a trial may not be the same as would be observed in clinical practice.

Blinding is particularly problematic for clinical interpretation of the noncompliance that often occurs in drug trials. When a trial subject chooses not to comply with the specified trial protocol, he makes this decision knowing only the probability that he is receiving each drug, not the actuality. Compliance may differ when the patient and clinician know what drug is being administered.

It has been common in study of trial data to perform intention-to-treat analysis, which examines the outcomes of assignment into a treatment group rather than the outcomes of receipt of treatment. Noncompliance is logically impossible in intention-to-treat analysis because subjects cannot modify their treatment assignments. This fact may tempt one to think that compliance need not be a concern in study of trial data. This temptation should be resisted. Intention-to-treat analysis does not predict how clinicians and patients would behave in practice, when they know the treatments prescribed.

Given that blinding may create problems in extrapolating from experimental to clinical treatments, why has blinding been standard procedure in the conduct of drug trials? Medical researchers sometimes assert that blinding is worthwhile because it enhances the internal validity of trials, even though it may reduce external validity. This reasoning is often phrased by asserting that standard trials aim to show the "efficacy" of treatments rather than the "effectiveness" and that blinding is helpful in showing efficacy. For example, Gartlehner et al. (2006) write:

> Clinicians and policymakers often distinguish between the efficacy and the effectiveness of an intervention. Efficacy trials (explanatory trials) determine whether an intervention produces the expected result under ideal circumstances. Effectiveness trials (pragmatic trials) measure the degree of beneficial effect under "real world" clinical settings. . . . Ensuring generalizability may compromise internal validity. Under everyday clinical settings, factors such as patient or doctor preferences, or patient-doctor relationships can influence response and compliance. Random allocation, allocation concealment, and blinding negate these factors, thereby increasing internal validity on the one hand and decreasing external validity on the other. (p. 3)

2.3. From Measured Outcomes to Patient Welfare

The treatments studied in trials may affect patient welfare in many ways. When treating a life-threatening health problem, the first outcome that may come to mind is life span, but it is rarely the only one. Whatever a patient's condition may be, life-threatening or not, treatments may have diverse effects on what is broadly called "quality of life."

Researchers performing trials must decide what outcomes to measure and how to assess multiple outcomes. I discuss prevailing practices that create difficulties in extrapolating trial findings to patient care.

INTERPRETING SURROGATE OUTCOMES

It would be ideal to measure all outcomes that may affect patient welfare, but this may be infeasible. A serious measurement problem often occurs when trials have short durations. Clinicians and patients want to learn long-term outcomes of treatments, but short trials reveal only short-run outcomes. Credible extrapolation from the surrogate outcomes measured in short trials to long-term outcomes of interest can be challenging.

Trials for drug approval by the FDA provide a good illustration. The longest, called *Phase 3 trials*, typically run for only two to three years. When these trials are not long enough to observe the health outcomes of real interest, the practice is to measure surrogate outcomes and base drug approval decisions on their values. For example, treatments for heart disease may be evaluated using data on patient cholesterol levels and blood pressure rather than data on heart attacks and life span. Thus, the trials used in drug approval only reveal the distribution of surrogate outcomes in the study population, not the distribution of outcomes of real health interest.

Some medical researchers have called attention to the difficulty of extrapolating from surrogate outcomes to health outcomes of interest in trials for drug approval. For example, Fleming and Demets (1996), who review the prevalent use of surrogate outcomes in Phase 3 trials evaluating drug treatments for heart disease, cancer, HIV/AIDS, osteoporosis, and other diseases, write: "Surrogate end points are rarely, if ever, adequate substitutes for the definitive clinical outcome in phase 3 trials" (p. 605). Considering approval of cancer drugs in the European Union by the European Medicines Agency (EMA), Davis et al. (2017, pp. 10–11) write:

> Most new oncology drugs authorised by the EMA in 2009–13 came onto the market without clear evidence that they improved the quality or

quantity of patients' lives, and, when survival gains over available treatment alternatives were shown, they were not always clinically meaningful. Little new information to guide patients, their treating clinicians, or decisions about whether or not to pay for treatments was generated in the postmarketing period. This situation has negative implications for patients and public health.

Considering approval of cancer drugs in the United States and Europe, Prasad (2017, p. 1) writes:

> Although we are approving cancer drugs at a rapid pace, few come to market with good evidence that they improve patient centred outcomes. If they do, they often offer marginal benefits that may be lost in the heterogeneous patients of the real world. Most approvals of cancer drugs are based on flimsy or untested surrogate endpoints, and postmarketing studies rarely validate the efficacy and safety of these drugs on patient centred endpoints. Add to this that the average cancer drug costs in excess of $100 000 (£75 000; €85 000) per year of treatment, and the conclusion seems that the regulatory system is broken.

Measurement of surrogate outcomes is also common in trials performed for research rather than drug approval. Consider trials of drug treatment for hypertension. The trial reported by Materson et al. (1993) followed subjects for only one year and evaluated alternative drugs by the reduction in blood pressure that they achieved rather than by significant health outcomes.

The Beckett, SHEP, and Staessen trials discussed in section 2.1 at first appear exemplary in that they measured important health outcomes, including the occurrence of strokes, major cardiovascular events, and deaths. However, the Beckett and Staessen trials followed most patients for no more than two years. The SHEP trial had a longer median duration of 4.5 years.

ASSESSING MULTIPLE OUTCOMES

Suppose that the designer of a trial can measure all the outcomes that may affect patient welfare. The utilitarian perspective on patient care recommends assessment of each treatment studied in the trial by the welfare that it yields. Welfare assessment combines the multiple outcomes of a treatment to determine its net potential impact on a patient. It recognizes that treatment choice may require making tradeoffs: One treatment may be better for a patient in some respects but worse in others. For example, we have previously observed that surveillance may be better than aggressive treatment if a patient is healthy but worse if the patient is ill.

The prevailing approach to reporting trial findings does not combine the multiple outcomes of a treatment to determine net impact. The standard protocol calls on the designer of a trial to a priori designate a single primary outcome (or endpoint) for the trial. The National Cancer Institute Dictionary of Cancer Terms defines the primary endpoint to be:

> The main result that is measured at the end of a study to see if a given treatment worked (e.g., the number of deaths or the difference in survival between the treatment group and the control group). What the primary endpoint will be is decided before the study begins.

Treatment outcomes other than the primary endpoint are called secondary outcomes and are given lesser attention when reporting trial findings. Adverse secondary outcomes on healthy tissue or organs are called "side effects" of the treatment. The FDA provides its perspective on primary and secondary endpoints in US Food and Drug Administration (2017a).

Making a sharp distinction between the primary endpoint and secondary outcomes is reasonable from a welfare perspective when the primary endpoint is the dominant determinant of patient welfare or, put another way, when there is little variation in secondary outcomes across treatments. It is not reasonable otherwise.

Consider trials assessing anticoagulation drugs such as warfarin as treatments for atrial fibrillation. It has been standard to designate the occurrence of stroke as the primary endpoint, with major bleeding viewed as a secondary outcome; see, for example, Boston Area Anticoagulation Trial for Atrial Fibrillation Investigators (1990) and Ezekowitz et al. (1992). However, the risk of serious bleeding with warfarin treatment has been thought sufficiently serious as to prompt strong warnings to patients. For example, a posting on the website of the Mayo Clinic declares (Mayo Clinic Staff, 2018): "Although commonly used to treat blood clots, warfarin . . . can have dangerous side effects or interactions that can place you at risk of bleeding."

From the perspective of patient welfare, it may be more appropriate to view occurrence of strokes and major bleeding as jointly relevant outcomes rather than to consider the former to be the primary outcome and the latter to be secondary. Thus, we may view a patient receiving warfarin as experiencing one of four possible outcomes: (1) neither stroke nor major bleeding, (2) stroke and no major bleeding, (3) major bleeding and no stroke, (4) both stroke and major bleeding. Which outcome will occur is not known at the time of treatment. The standard recommendation of medical economics would be to determine the probability that each outcome will occur, multiply this probability by patient utility in the event of this outcome, and use expected utility to measure patient welfare.

2.4. From Hypothesis Tests to Treatment Decisions

I have so far called attention to how the performance of trials can make it difficult to extrapolate trial findings to clinical practice. Further difficulties stem from use of questionable statistical methods to analyze trial outcomes. I discuss the use of hypothesis testing and meta-analysis in this section and the next.

USING HYPOTHESIS TESTS TO COMPARE TREATMENTS

It has been a long-standing practice to use trial data to test a specified null hypothesis against an alternative and to use the outcome of the test to compare treatments. A common procedure when comparing two treatments is to view one as the status quo and the other as an innovation. The usual null hypothesis is that the innovation is no better than the status quo, and the alternative is that the innovation is better. If the null hypothesis is not rejected, it is recommended that the status quo treatment be used in clinical practice. If the null is rejected, it is recommended that the innovation be the treatment of choice.

The standard practice has been to perform a test that fixes the probability of rejecting the null hypothesis when it is correct, called the probability of a Type I error. Then sample size determines the probability of rejecting the alternative hypothesis when it is correct, called the probability of a Type II error. The power of a test is defined as one minus the probability of a Type II error. The convention has been to choose a trial sample size that yields specified power at a value of the effect size deemed clinically important.

The FDA uses such a test to approve new treatments. A firm that is seeking approval of a new drug or medical device (the innovation) performs trials that compare the innovation with an approved treatment or placebo (the status quo). US Food and Drug Administration (2014), which provides guidance for the design of randomized controlled trials (RCTs) to evaluate new medical devices, states that the probability of a Type I error is conventionally set to 0.05 and that the probability of a Type II error depends on the claim for the device but should not exceed 0.20. The International Conference on

Harmonisation (1999) provides similar guidance for the design and conduct of trials evaluating pharmaceuticals, stating:

> Conventionally the probability of type I error is set at 5% or less or as dictated by any adjustments made necessary for multiplicity considerations; the precise choice may be influenced by the prior plausibility of the hypothesis under test and the desired impact of the results. The probability of type II error is conventionally set at 10% to 20%. (p. 1923)

Manski and Tetenov (2016) observe that there are several reasons why hypothesis testing may yield unsatisfactory results for medical decisions. These include:

Use of Conventional Asymmetric Error Probabilities

It has been standard to fix the probability of Type I error at 5% and the probability of Type II error at 10–20%. The theory of hypothesis testing gives no rationale for selection of these conventional error probabilities. It gives no reason why a clinician concerned with patient welfare should find it reasonable to make treatment choices that have a substantially greater probability of Type II than Type I error.

Inattention to Magnitudes of Losses When Errors Occur

A clinician should care about more than the probabilities of Type I and II error. He should care as well about the magnitudes of the losses to patient welfare that arise when errors occur. A given error probability should be less acceptable when the welfare difference between treatments is larger, but the theory of hypothesis testing does not take this into account.

Limitation to Settings with Two Treatments

A clinician often chooses among several treatments, and many clinical trials compare more than two treatments. Yet the standard theory of hypothesis testing only contemplates choice between two treatments. Statisticians have struggled to extend it to deal sensibly with comparisons of multiple treatments. See, for example, Dunnett (1955) and Cook and Farewell (1996).

The third issue is well-appreciated, but the first two are often overlooked. A simple example shows why they may matter for patient care.

Example

Suppose that a typically terminal form of cancer may be treated by a status quo treatment or an innovation. It is known from experience that mean patient life span with the status quo treatment is one year. Prior to use of the innovation, medical researchers see two possibilities for its effectiveness. It may be less effective than the status quo, yielding a mean life span of only one-third of a year, or it may be much more effective, yielding a mean life span of 5 years.

Suppose that a randomized trial is performed to learn the effectiveness of the innovation. Let the trial data be used to perform a conventional hypothesis test comparing the innovation and the status quo. The null hypothesis is that the innovation is no more effective than the status quo and the alternative is that the innovation is more effective. The probability of a Type I error is set at 0.05 and that of a Type II error is 0.20. The test result is used to choose between the treatments.

A Type I error occurs with frequentist probability 0.05 and reduces mean patient life span by two-thirds of a year (1 year minus 1/3 year). A Type II error occurs with frequentist probability 0.20 and reduces mean patient life span by 4 years (5 years minus 1 year). Thus, use of the test to choose between the status quo and the innovation implies that society is willing to tolerate a large (0.20) chance of a large welfare loss (4 years) when making a Type II error, but only a small (0.05) chance of a small welfare loss (2/3 of a year) when making a Type I error. The theory of hypothesis testing does not motivate this asymmetry.

USING HYPOTHESIS TESTS TO CHOOSE WHEN TO REPORT FINDINGS

Beyond its use to choose between treatments, hypothesis testing is also used to determine when research articles should report trial findings conditional on observed patient attributes. Chapter 1 showed that optimal patient care segments patients into attribute groups and maximizes expected utility within each group. Clinicians commonly have much information—medical histories, findings from screening and diagnostic tests, and demographic attributes—about the patients they treat. Yet the medical journal articles that report on trials typically present trial findings aggregated to broad demographic groups.

For example, Crits-Christoph et al. (1999) report on a trial that places cocaine-dependent patients in one of four treatment groups, each designated treatment combining group drug counseling (GDC) with another form of therapy. The article provides much descriptive information on subject attributes including race, sex, age, education, employment status, type and severity of drug use, psychiatric state, and personality. Yet the article does not report treatment outcomes conditional on any of these patient attributes. Indeed, its conclusion section makes no reference to the possibility that treatment response might vary with attributes, stating simply: "Compared with professional psychotherapy, a manual-guided combination of intensive individual drug counseling and GDC has promise for the treatment of cocaine dependence" (p. 493).

Conventional ideas about what constitutes adequate statistical precision for an empirical finding to be of interest have been strongly influenced by the theory of hypothesis testing. Conditioning on attributes generally reduces the statistical precision of estimates of treatment effects, to the point where findings become "statistically insignificant." Aiming to avoid publication of statistically insignificant results ex ante, researchers often report findings only for groups whose sample sizes are large enough to perform tests with conventional Type I and II error probabilities. Moreover, researchers sometimes selectively report findings that are statistically significant ex post by standard criteria. This reporting practice has been recognized to generate publication bias (Ioannidis, 2005; Wasserstein and Lazar, 2016).

If researchers want to inform patient care, they should not view statistical insignificance as a reason to refrain from studying and reporting observable heterogeneity in treatment response. Clinicians should be concerned with the quantitative variation of outcomes with treatments and attributes. Hypothesis tests do not address this question. Subject to considerations of subject confidentiality and space constraints, research journals should encourage publication of findings conditional on observed patient attributes. When space constraints prevent publication of all potentially informative findings, researchers may report them on the Internet or through other means.

2.5. Wishful Meta-Analyses of Disparate Studies

The problems discussed above relate to analysis of findings from single trials. Further difficulties arise when researchers and guideline developers attempt to combine findings from multiple trials. It is easy to understand the impetus to combine findings. Decision makers must somehow interpret the mass of information provided by evidence-based research. The hard question is how to interpret this information sensibly.

Combination of findings is often performed by *systematic review* of a set of studies. This is a subjective process, akin to exercise of clinical judgment.

For example, James et al. (2014) describes how the JNC 8 team combined the information in dozens of trials on treatment for hypertension. The authors write:

> An external methodology team performed the literature review, summarized data from selected papers into evidence tables, and provided a summary of the evidence. From this evidence review, the panel crafted evidence statements and voted on agreement or disagreement with each statement. For approved evidence statements, the panel then voted on the quality of the evidence. . . . The panel attempted to achieve 100% consensus whenever possible, but a two-thirds majority was considered acceptable. (p. 509)

Statisticians have proposed *meta-analysis* in an effort to provide an objective methodology for combining the findings of multiple studies. Meta-analysis was originally developed to address a purely statistical problem. One wants to estimate as well as possible some parameter characterizing a study population. Often the parameter of interest is the mean health outcome that would occur if all members of the population were to receive a specified treatment.

Suppose that multiple independent trials have been performed on the same study population, each drawing a random sample from the population. If the raw data on the trial outcomes are available, the most precise way to estimate the parameter integrates the samples and computes the estimate using all the data. Suppose, however, that the raw data are unavailable, making it infeasible to combine the samples. Instead, multiple parameter estimates may be available, each computed with the data from a different sample. Meta-analysis proposes methods to combine the multiple estimates. The usual proposal is to compute a weighted average of the estimates, the weights varying with sample size.

The original concept of meta-analysis is uncontroversial, but its applicability is limited. It is rarely the case that multiple independent trials are performed on the same population. It is more common for multiple trials to be performed on distinct patient populations that may have different distributions of treatment response. The protocols for administration of treatments and the measurement of outcomes may vary across trials as well. Meta-analyses are performed often in such settings, computing weighted averages of estimates for distinct study populations and trial designs.

The problem is that it may not be clear how to define and interpret a weighted average of the separate estimates. Meta-analyses often answer these questions through the lens of a *random-effects* model (DerSimonian and Laird, 1986). The model assumes that each of the multiple estimates pertains to a distinct parameter value drawn at random from a population of potential parameter values. Then a weighted average of the estimates is interpreted to be an estimate of the mean of all potential parameter values.

A META-ANALYSIS OF OUTCOMES OF BARIATRIC SURGERY

Medical researchers have used random-effects models to perform numerous meta-analyses of studies evaluating treatments for many diseases. To illustrate, consider Buchwald et al. (2004), who used this approach to combine the findings of 134 studies of the outcomes of bariatric surgery. The 134 studies included five randomized trials enrolling 621 patients and 28 nonrandomized but somehow otherwise controlled trials enrolling 4,613 patients. The 101 other studies, described as "uncontrolled case series," involved 16,860 patients. The studies were performed around the world, fifty-eight with European patients, fifty-six with North American patients, and twenty with patients from elsewhere. The studies followed patients for different periods of time. They measured weight loss, a primary health outcome of interest, in multiple ways.

To summarize the findings of the meta-analysis, the authors write: "The mean (95% confidence interval) percentage of excess weight loss was 61.2% (58.1%–64.4%) for all patients" (Buchwald et al., 2004, p. 1724). The estimated mean of 61.2 percent considers the 134 studies to be a sample drawn from a population of potential studies. It is not clear what implications should be drawn by a clinician who treats a population of patients, not a population of studies.

THE MISLEADING RHETORIC OF META-ANALYSIS

Unfortunately, the relevance to clinical practice of a weighted average of estimates is often obscure. DerSimonian and Laird consider each of the trials considered in a meta-analysis to be drawn at random "from a population of possible studies" (1986, p. 181). They interpret the weighted average of estimates computed in the meta-analysis as an estimate of the mean health outcome across the postulated population of possible studies. However, they do not explain what is meant by a population of possible studies, nor why the published studies should be considered a random sample from this population. Even if these concepts are meaningful, they do not explain how a mean outcome across a population of possible studies connects to what should matter to a clinician, namely the mean health outcome across the relevant population of patients.

Medical researchers who have performed meta-analyses using the DerSimonian and Laird random-effects model have struggled to explain coherently how clinicians should use the findings. Consider, for example, the meta-analysis performed by Chen and Parmigiani (2007) of ten disparate studies predicting risk of breast and ovarian cancer among women who carry BRCA mutations. The authors describe a weighted average of the risks reported by all studies as a "consensus estimate" (p. 1331). However, there is no consensus across studies, which report heterogeneous estimates pertaining to heterogeneous populations.

Chen and Parmigiani conclude their article with this guidance to clinicians:

> In current clinical practice, two scenarios are possible. In the first, the clinician is able to identify a single study that matches the relevant patient population for his or her practice. In the second, which is perhaps more common, there is no clear criterion for deciding which study is most appropriate for a particular patient. In this case, given current knowledge, a meta-analysis that acknowledges heterogeneity is the most evidence-based and, arguably, ethically sound approach to risk counseling. (2007, p. 1333)

Although meta-analysis is "evidence-based," this descriptor should not reassure clinicians. What matters is whether a methodology uses available evidence reasonably.

Some researchers have sought to go beyond meta-analysis by exploring how study findings vary with observed attributes of the studies. *Meta-regression* uses standard regression approaches, viewing study findings as outcomes and features of study designs as covariates (e.g., Stanley and Jarrell, 1989; Thompson and Higgins, 2002). Meta-regressions document the association between study designs and findings, but their usefulness in informing clinical practice is unclear.

THE ALGEBRAIC WISDOM OF CROWDS

Empirical researchers who study prediction in various fields of science have long reported that the mean of a set of predictions is more accurate than the individual predictions used to form the mean. Formally, they report that the prediction error of the mean prediction is smaller than the average prediction error across the individual predictions. Surowiecki (2004) calls this phenomenon the "wisdom of crowds." A review article by Clemen (1989) put it this way:

> The results have been virtually unanimous: combining multiple forecasts leads to increased forecast accuracy. This has been the result whether the forecasts are judgmental or statistical, econometric or extrapolation. Furthermore, in many cases one can make dramatic performance improvements by simply averaging the forecasts. (p. 559)

Citing this literature, one may be tempted to hope that, however deficient the logic of meta-analysis may be, the methodology may work in practice. I strongly caution against this.

McNees (1992) and Manski (2011, 2016) show that the wisdom of crowds is not an empirical regularity. It is rather an algebraic result that holds whenever the loss function used to measure prediction error is such that one suffers an increasing marginal loss as the magnitude of the error grows. In the language of mathematics, such a loss function is *convex*. Prominent examples of convex loss functions, used routinely in studies of predictive accuracy, are square and absolute loss functions.

With a convex loss function, the result known as the wisdom of crowds holds as a result of the theorem known as Jensen's Inequality. It holds regardless of whether one combines predictions by their simple mean or by a weighted average. Being an algebraic property rather than an empirical regularity, the result holds regardless of the quality of the individual predictions that are combined. Thus, a weighted mean prediction need not perform well in an absolute sense. It may be a good prediction or a terrible one.

2.6. Sacrificing Relevance for Certitude

Researchers often are aware that they cannot form a credible risk assessment or prediction of treatment response that informs patient care. Rather than express uncertainty, they may change the objective and report findings that are credible but not clinically relevant. Thus, they sacrifice relevance for certitude. Leading examples in medical research are the focus on internal validity when reporting randomized trials and the performance of meta-analysis of disparate studies. Complement 2A presents another example, the use of odds ratios computed in retrospective studies to measure health risks. Manski (2019a) provides a broad discussion, citing nonmedical examples.

Notable scientists have critiqued this common practice. The statistician John Tukey wrote (1962, pp. 13–14): "Far better an approximate answer to the right question, which is often vague, than an exact answer to the wrong question, which can always be made precise." Many cite some version of the joke about the drunk and the lamppost. Noam Chomsky has been quoted as putting it this way (Barsky, 1998, p. 95): "Science is a bit like the joke about the drunk who is looking under a lamppost for a key that he has lost on the other side of the street, because that's where the light is."

Sacrificing relevance for certitude may be relatively harmless if everyone understands that the quantity being estimated or predicted is not of clinical interest. The problem is that authors may not be forthright about this, or readers may misinterpret findings.

3

Credible Use of Evidence to Inform Patient Care

The questionable methodological practices described in chapter 2 have become prevalent largely because evidence-based medical research, with its strong emphasis on randomized trials, has valued internal validity over external validity. A consequence has been wishful extrapolation from trials to patient care.

Research can better inform care if it seeks to provide knowledge that promotes effective decision making. Optimal personalized care, as formalized by medical economists, assigns treatments that maximize patients' welfare conditional on their observed attributes. From this perspective, studies of treatment response are useful to the degree that they reveal how welfare varies with treatments and patient attributes.

Methodological research should aim to determine the information relevant to patient care that studies provide, when evidence is combined with credible assumptions. I remarked in the introduction that statistical imprecision and identification problems limit the informativeness of studies. Statistical imprecision stems from small sample size. Identification problems are the difficulties that persist when sample size grows without bound.

Statistical imprecision may be vexing, but identification is the more fundamental challenge. This chapter discusses how identification problems arise and summarizes econometric research that studies their form and severity. Chapter 5 will address statistical imprecision, discussing decision criteria for reasonable treatment choice with trial data.

I begin broadly, describing common identification problems that arise when studying trial or observational data. I then discuss econometric research that analyzes these problems.

3.1. Identification of Treatment Response

UNOBSERVABILITY OF COUNTERFACTUAL TREATMENT OUTCOMES

Perhaps the most fundamental identification problem in analysis of treatment response stems from the unobservability of *counterfactual* treatment outcomes. Counterfactuals are outcomes that patients would have experienced if they had received treatments other than those they received. In principle, observation of a study population can reveal the outcomes that patients realize with the treatments they receive. Observation cannot answer "what if?" questions; that is, what would have happened if patients had received other treatments. To make optimal treatment choices requires comparison of potential outcomes under alternative treatments. Hence, the evidence available to medical research inevitably is incomplete.

To illustrate, consider a study population of patients who have been diagnosed with a localized cancer, which has been removed surgically. Suppose that each patient may now be cared for by surveillance alone (treatment A) or by surveillance plus one of several adjuvant therapies: chemotherapy (treatment B), radiation (treatment C), or chemotherapy and radiation (treatment D). Alternatives A through D are mutually exclusive—each patient in a study population can receive only one of the four. A patient's outcome with the treatment he receives may be observable, but the three counterfactual outcomes are unobservable.

The unobservability of counterfactual outcomes is a matter of universal logic. The logic holds in randomized trials and observational studies alike. The problem is not resolvable by increasing sample size or by collection of richer data. It is a basic aspect of empirical inference that can be mitigated only by making credible assumptions that relate observed and counterfactual outcomes.

TRIAL DATA

Researchers often draw a sharp distinction between observational studies and trials, asserting that the unobservability of counterfactual outcomes poses a problem for interpretation of the former but not the latter. The foundation for this distinction is an assumption that is credible in trials with perfect compliance. Assume that the patients in a large study population are randomly assigned to treatments and they all comply with their assigned treatments. Then the distribution of treatment response in the overall study population is replicated in the subpopulation who receive each treatment. This conclusion does not hold precisely when trials are performed on samples of finite size, but statistical imprecision diminishes as sample size increases.

It is essential to understand that the assumption of random treatment assignment does not render observable the counterfactual outcomes of the patients in a trial. What it does do is provide a credible way to make probabilistic predictions of the outcomes that would occur if the study population were to receive alternative treatments. One observes the actual distribution of outcomes for the patients in the trial who received a specified treatment and uses this to predict the distribution of outcomes that would occur if the treatment were to be assigned to the entire study population. The credibility of this prediction underlies the common remark that trials are the "gold standard" for analysis of treatment response.

While trials are informative, the assumption of random assignment does not reveal all that clinicians and patients might like to learn about treatment response. Consider a patient who asks: "What is the chance that I will live longer with treatment A than with treatment B?" A trial comparing A and B would enable one to answer this question if one could observe how long each patient in the trial would live with each treatment. But each patient in the trial receives only one of the two treatments, so only one of the two outcomes is observable. See Mullahy (2018) for a formal analysis. He explains that trial data do not yield a precise answer to the patient's question, but they do imply a bound on the probability that the patient will live longer with treatment A.

OBSERVATIONAL DATA

Now consider observational studies. It typically is not credible to assume random treatment allocation when clinicians choose the treatments that patients receive. Nor may it be credible to make another assumption that enables precise probabilistic prediction of counterfactual outcomes. Hence, it is common to view the unobservability of counterfactual outcomes as a problem that afflicts observational studies but not trials with perfect compliance.

When cautioning against the use of observational data to analyze treatment response, medical researchers and guideline developers commonly use qualitative rather than quantitative terms. The *Cochrane Handbook* states (Higgins and Green, 2011, sec. 5.5): "the extent, and even the direction, of the bias is difficult to predict." Later, when introducing a tool for assessing "risk of bias," the *Handbook* authors write (sec. 8.3.1): "Because it is impossible to know the extent of bias (or even the true risk of bias) in a given study, the possibility of validating any proposed tool is limited." Elsewhere, the authors of the JNC 8 guidelines for treatment of hypertension state (James et al., 2014, p. 508): "The panel limited its evidence review to RCTs because they are less subject to bias than other study designs."

These and similar cautions reflect a perception that it is not possible to characterize quantitatively the severity of the identification problem created by the unobservability of counterfactual outcomes. Hence, writers think that the safest course is to downplay observational data or disregard them entirely.

In fact, the unobservability of counterfactual outcomes affects inference with observational data in a simple way. Section 3.5 of this chapter will show that observational data yield quantifiable partial conclusions about treatment response even without any knowledge of the process used to allocate treatments. Sections 3.5 through 3.7 will show how to obtain tighter partial conclusions by combining observational data with various credible assumptions.

Interestingly, discussions of observational studies in the literature on evidence-based medicine rarely use the term *identification*. Instead, writers express concern with the *bias* of estimates of treatment effects obtained with observational data. Examples are the passages quoted above from Higgins and Green (2011) and James et al. (2014).

In statistical theory, a sample estimate of a population treatment effect is said to have bias if the average value of the estimate, computed across repeated samples, does not equal the population effect. Bias stems from statistical imprecision alone if, as sample size increases, the average value of the estimate converges to the population effect. When the treatment effect is partially identified, there generally exists no estimate whose bias disappears as sample size increases.

Clearly it is identification rather than imprecision that prompted the *Cochrane Handbook* and the JNC 8 to disparage observational studies. If imprecision had been their concern, the *Handbook* and the JNC 8 could have recommended use of observational studies that have sufficiently large samples. However, having access to "big data" would not reduce concern about the bias of estimates of treatment effects obtained with observational data.

TRIALS WITH IMPERFECT COMPLIANCE

Having discussed trials with perfect compliance and observational studies, it remains to consider trials with imperfect compliance. Such trials share with observational studies the difficulty that it may not be credible to assume that treatment allocation is random. When patients choose whether to comply with assigned treatments, they need not do so randomly.

Much research on evidence-based medicine avoids consideration of imperfect compliance by performing intention-to-treat analysis. As noted in chapter 2, such analysis does not solve the identification problem generated by noncompliance. It just makes it appear in a different form, namely that of an extrapolation problem. The trial enables one to predict outcomes when patients are offered treatments in the setting of a trial. To inform patient care, we want to predict outcomes when patients are offered treatments in clinical practice.

EXTRAPOLATION PROBLEMS

The foregoing discussion concerned identification of treatment response within a study population. Chapter 2 discussed several further difficulties that may arise when one attempts to extrapolate trial findings to patient care. I called attention to the difficulty of extrapolating credibly from study populations to patient populations, from experimental treatments to clinical treatments, and from measured outcomes to patient welfare. Extrapolation is an identification problem, not a matter of statistical imprecision. Increasing the sample sizes of trials would increase the precision of their findings, but it would not improve the credibility of extrapolations.

Extrapolation from observational studies may also be problematic. Study populations may differ from the patient populations that clinicians will treat. Studies with short follow-up periods may measure surrogate outcomes rather than health outcomes of intrinsic interest. Nevertheless, I think it broadly correct to say that extrapolation from observational studies tends to pose a less severe problem than does extrapolation from trials.

Recall that the study populations in trials are composed of volunteers and commonly exclude persons with comorbidities. In contrast, observational

studies often collect data from broad study populations like the populations that clinicians treat. Recall that trials typically monitor patients more
intensively than in practice and that drug trials use a double-blind protocol
that prevents clinicians and patients from knowing what treatments subjects
receive. In contrast, observational studies enable one to learn the outcomes
of patient care as it occurs in practice.

MISSING DATA AND MEASUREMENT ERRORS

Beyond the unobservability of counterfactual outcomes and extrapolation
problems, analysis of trial and observational data may confront difficulties
generated by missing data and measurement errors. Outcome and/or attribute data may be missing for patients who drop out of trials or who do not
respond to surveys in observational studies. When patient outcome and
attribute data are collected, measurement may not be accurate.

Missing data and measurement errors generate identification problems.
Increasing sample size does not diminish the severity of the issues. The only
ways to mitigate them are to improve the quality of data collection or to
make credible assumptions that have identifying power.

3.2. Studying Identification

Although identification problems are ubiquitous in analysis of treatment
response, they are given little attention in the textbooks and articles that
have provided the standard methodological framework for evidence-based
medical research. These sources commonly focus on statistical imprecision
and provide informal discussions of bias. As a result, medical researchers,
guideline developers, and clinicians may have little quantitative sense of how
identification problems affect inference.

Study of identification has been a core concern of research in econometrics, from the beginnings of the field in the 1930s through the present.
For about fifty years, the literature focused on identification of systems of
linear simultaneous equations and was most famously applied to analyze
transactions in competitive markets. This early research can also be used to
analyze treatment response with observational data, when treatments vary
in the magnitude of their dose. However, it is not applicable to comparison
of qualitatively different treatments, which has been the prevalent concern of
evidence-based medicine. Hence, it is not surprising that econometricians and
medical researchers long found little reason to communicate with one another.

The prospects for beneficial communication have grown substantially from the 1990s onward, as econometricians have increasingly studied identification of response to qualitatively different treatments, using either observational or trial data. The recent econometric research has multiple branches, whose differing objectives affect the features of treatment response that authors want to learn. An especially sharp distinction separates research that aims to learn the magnitudes of treatment effects within certain subsets of study populations from research that studies treatment response to inform prospective treatment decisions in patient populations. The latter objective motivates my research and this book.

Studying identification of treatment response when available data are combined with credible assumptions, I have found that empirical research may yield informative bounds but typically does not yield exact findings. Thus, treatment response is *partially identified* rather than *point-identified*. The practical task of econometric research has been to characterize the identified bounds in a tractable manner. This done, guideline developers and clinicians should be able to use the findings.

For example, as I suggested in the introduction, they may be able to provide credible bounds to patients who ask: "What is the chance that I will develop disease X in the next five years?" or "What is the chance that treatment Y will cure me?"

My research has studied use of observational and trial data. Both types of data can be informative to some degree, so analysis of both should be encouraged. The identification problems associated with trial data may be more or less severe than those that arise with observational data, depending on the context. I caution against broad statements that praise trials as "the gold standard" or that disparage observational studies.

To go beyond generalities, the remainder of this chapter describes research on identification that I think should help to inform patient care. The discussions below suggest potential clinical uses of the findings obtained to date, but I will not claim that these findings provide comprehensive guidance. Study of identification intended to inform patient care is a work in progress.

3.3. Identification with Missing Data on Patient Outcomes or Attributes

Missing data on patient outcomes and attributes is a frequent occurrence in both trials and observational studies. Researchers commonly assume that data are missing at random, in the sense that the observability of an outcome or attribute is statistically independent of its value. This done, researchers often report findings only for sampled patients with complete data, discarding those with incomplete data. Or they impute missing values and report findings for all patients, acting as if the imputed values of missing data are actual values. Either way, researchers report point estimates of treatment effects.

Assuming that data are missing at random superficially solves the identification problem created by missingness. I say "superficially" because it is rare for researchers to discuss the credibility of the assumption. They typically invoke it without much if any comment. Yet, there often is reason to worry that the assumption is unrealistic.

In a sequence of analyses, I have sought to understand how missing data might affect the conclusions drawn in empirical research. I have found it useful to begin by asking what one can learn about treatment response in the absence of any knowledge of the process generating missing data. Conclusions drawn in this manner are weaker but more credible than those drawn by assuming that data are missing at random or by making another assumption. Thus, analysis of inference with missing data illustrates the *Law of Decreasing Credibility* mentioned in the introduction; that is, the credibility of inference decreases with the strength of the assumptions maintained.

Inference without assumptions about the nature of missing data basically is a matter of contemplating all possible configurations of the missing data. Doing so generates the set of possible conclusions in empirical research, called the *identification region* or the *identified set*. The practical challenge when performing identification analysis is to characterize this set of possible conclusions in a tractable way, so applied researchers can use the findings.

Manski (1989, 1990b, 1994) show that analysis is simple when only outcome data are missing. The most transparent case occurs when the objective is to learn the success probability for a treatment when the outcome of interest is binary (success or failure). Then the smallest and largest possible values of the success probability are determined by conjecturing that all missing outcomes are failures or successes, respectively.

The same reasoning holds when the outcome of interest is a patient's remaining life span and the objective is to learn the mean or median outcome that a treatment yields in the patient population. Then the smallest and largest possible values of the mean or median are determined by conjecturing that all patients with missing outcomes die immediately or live as long as is humanly possible.

Analysis is more complex when some sample members may have missing outcome data, some may have missing attribute data, and some may have jointly missing outcome and attribute data. Horowitz and Manski (1998, 2000) study these settings. The latter article provides an illustrative application to a trial of treatments for hypertension, which I describe below.

MISSING DATA IN A TRIAL OF TREATMENTS
FOR HYPERTENSION

Horowitz and Manski (2000) analyzed identification of treatment response when a trial is performed but some patient outcome or attribute data are missing. Focusing on cases in which outcomes are binary (success or failure), we derived sharp bounds on success probabilities without imposing any assumptions about the distribution of the missing data. This analysis contrasts sharply with the conventional practice in medical research, which assumes that missing data are missing at random or have some other structure.

We applied the findings to data from a trial comparing treatments for hypertension. Materson et al. (1993) reported on a trial comparing treatments for hypertension sponsored by the US Department of Veteran Affairs (DVA). Male veteran patients at fifteen DVA hospitals were randomly assigned to one of six antihypertensive drug treatments or to placebo: hydrochlorothiazide ($t = 1$), atenolol ($t = 2$), captopril ($t = 3$), clonidine ($t = 4$), diltiazem ($t = 5$), prazosin ($t = 6$), placebo ($t = 7$). The trial had two phases. In the first, the dosage that brought diastolic blood pressure (DBP) below 90 mmHg was determined. In the second, it was determined whether DBP could be kept below 95 mmHg for a period. Treatment was defined to be successful if DBP < 90 mmHg on two consecutive measurement occasions in the first phase and DBP ≤ 95 mmHg in the second. Treatment was deemed unsuccessful otherwise. Thus, the measured outcome was binary, with $y = 1$ if the criterion for success was met and $y = 0$ otherwise. Materson et al. (1993) recommended that clinicians treating hypertension should consider this outcome as well as patient's quality of life and the cost of treatment.

The Materson et al. (1993) article examined how treatment response varies with the race and age of the patient. There were no missing data on these attributes. The authors performed an intention-to-treat analysis that interpreted attrition from the trial (also known as loss to follow-up) as lack of success; from this perspective there were no missing outcome data

TABLE 3.1. Missing Data in the DVA Hypertension Trial

Treatment	Number Randomized	Observed Successes	None Missing	Missing Only y	Missing Only x	Missing (y, x)
1	188	100	173	4	11	0
2	178	106	158	11	9	0
3	188	96	169	6	13	0
4	178	110	159	5	13	1
5	185	130	164	6	14	1
6	188	97	164	12	10	2
7	187	57	178	3	6	0

either. Horowitz and Manski (2000) obtained the trial data and used them to examine how treatment response varies with another attribute that does have missing data. This is the biochemical indicator "renin response," taking the values x = (low, medium, high), which had previously been studied as a factor that might be related to successful treatment (Freis, Materson, and Flamenbaum, 1983). Renin response was measured at the time of randomization, but data were missing for some subjects in the trial. Horowitz and Manski also removed the intention-to-treat interpretation of attrition as lack of success. Instead, we viewed subjects who leave the trial as having missing outcome data. The pattern of missing attribute and outcome data is shown in table 1 of Horowitz and Manski (2000), reproduced in table 3.1.

Horowitz and Manski (2000) used the identification analysis to estimate sharp bounds on the success probabilities for the seven treatments without imposing assumptions on the distribution of missing data. Rather than report the bounds on the success probabilities directly, the article reported the implied bounds on average treatment effects, which measure the efficacy of each treatment relative to the placebo. Table 3.2 shows the estimates of the bounds on the success probabilities themselves, which have previously been reported in Manski (2008).

To focus on the identification problem, ignore sampling imprecision and suppose that the estimates are population bounds rather than estimates of the bounds. Observe that even though the findings are bounds rather than precise success probabilities, many bounds are sufficiently narrow to enable one to conclude that certain treatments are dominated; that is, surely inferior to others. For patients with low renin response, treatments 1, 2, 3, 4, 6, and 7 are all dominated by treatment 5, which has the greatest lower

TABLE 3.2. Bounds on Success Probabilities Conditional on Renin Response

Renin Response	Treatment						
	1	2	3	4	5	6	7
Low	[0.54, 0.61]	[0.52, 0.62]	[0.43, 0.53]	[0.58, 0.66]	[0.66, 0.76]	[0.54, 0.65]	[0.29, 0.32]
Medium	[0.47, 0.62]	[0.60, 0.74]	[0.53, 0.68]	[0.50, 0.69]	[0.68, 0.85]	[0.41, 0.65]	[0.27, 0.32]
High	[0.28, 0.50]	[0.64, 0.86]	[0.56, 0.75]	[0.63, 0.84]	[0.55, 0.78]	[0.34, 0.59]	[0.28, 0.40]

bound (0.66). For patients with medium renin response, treatments 1, 3, 6, and 7 are dominated by treatment 5, which again has the greatest lowest bound (0.68). For patients with high renin response, treatments 1, 6, and 7 are dominated by treatment 2, which has the greatest lowest bound (0.64). Thus, without imposing any assumptions on the distribution of missing data, a clinician can reject treatments 1, 6, and 7 for all patients, reject treatment 3 for patients with medium renin response, and determine that treatment 5 is optimal for patients with low renin response.

The analysis of Horowitz and Manski (2000) shows that missing data in the DVA trial lowers its internal validity but does not eliminate it. Materson et al. (1993) may or may not have been correct to assume that treatment failed for all patients with missing outcomes. Data on renin response may or may not have been missing at random. The bounds on success probabilities presented in table 3.2 give the conclusions that hold without making these or other assumptions about the missing data. Hence, the bounds quantify the degree to which the DVA trial is internally valid, despite the presence of missing data.

It is important to keep in mind that internal validity does not imply external validity. The DVA trial was performed on a study population that differs from the patient populations that many clinicians treat. The trial used the standard protocol of double-blinding assigned treatments. The measured outcome—whether DBP is lower than a specified threshold after a period—is a surrogate rather than an outcome of real health interest.

MISSING DATA ON FAMILY SIZE WHEN PREDICTING GENETIC MUTATIONS

Partial identification analysis of the type performed by Horowitz and Manski and as illustrated in table 3.2 can quantify the potential severity of many missing data problems that occur in research on treatment response and risk assessment. Consider, for example, prediction of the risk that a woman with observed family history carries a gene mutation that makes development of breast cancer likely. This type of risk assessment has been used to develop probabilistic thresholds for recommendations that women should be referred for genetic testing. See American Society of Clinical Oncology (2018) for a listing of a set of risk evaluation models available to assist clinicians in deciding when patients should undergo genetic testing.

Amir et al. (2010) review existing risk assessment models and write:

> Because genetic testing for *BRCA1* and *BRCA2* mutations costs approximately $3000, insurance companies and health-care systems require a mutation carrier probability threshold for test use. In the United Kingdom, this threshold is set at a mutation carrier probability of 20%; in most of the rest of Europe and North America, the threshold is 10%. (p. 683)

The presumption when setting thresholds of 10% or 20% for referral to genetic testing is that the probabilistic predictions provided in the medical research literature are precise. However, missing data on family history make this presumption suspect.

Amir et al. (2010) verbally acknowledge difficulties in obtaining data on of family histories. As they explain:

> All risk assessment models have limitations: Adoption, small family size . . . , and lack of information about family history reduce the usefulness of all models to some degree. It is known that because of the reluctance of people to discuss their medical conditions, particularly those involving cancer, generations of family medical history are lost to present-day patients who are receiving care in the era of genetic testing. . . . There is therefore a need to improve methods for collecting and acknowledging family history even while risk models continue to have their accuracy improved. (pp. 683–684)

This verbal caution is welcome, but it is not clear how clinicians might use it. On the one hand, insurance companies and health-care systems set precise probabilistic thresholds for referral of patients to genetic testing. On the other hand, Amir et al. warn that the precise probabilistic predictions made by existing risk assessment models may be inaccurate to an unknown degree. Partial identification analysis can quantify the potential implications of the missing data problem that Amir et al. acknowledge.

3.4. Partial Personalized Risk Assessment

An extreme case of missing attribute data occurs when evidence-based predictions of disease risk or treatment response condition on a subset of the patient attributes that clinicians observe. Then data on the attributes not used in evidence-based research are entirely missing. This problem occurs regularly in both trials and observational studies. As discussed in chapter 1, clinicians have used subjective judgment to predict patient outcomes conditional on all observed patient attributes. However, psychologists have found that these judgments are fallible.

Manski (2018a) shows that this severe identification problem can be mitigated if the predictions made by evidence-based studies can be combined with auxiliary data that reveal the distribution of the missing attributes across the patient population. Sources of such auxiliary data sometimes exist. I illustrate below and complement 3A elaborates.

PREDICTING MEAN REMAINING LIFE SPAN

A common problem in health risk assessment is to predict remaining life span conditional on observed patient attributes. Life tables from the Centers for Disease Control provide actuarial predictions of life span in the United States conditional on (age, sex, race); see Arias (2015). However, the life tables do not predict life span conditional on other patient attributes that clinicians may observe. For example, clinicians readily observe patient blood pressure.

A clinician may want to predict the mean remaining life span for a patient with a certain (age, sex, race, blood pressure), but the life tables alone do not provide an evidence-based prediction. Manski (2018a) shows that one can bound mean remaining life span conditional on (age, sex, race, blood pressure) if one combines the evidence in the life tables with auxiliary data on the distribution of blood pressure among persons with the specified (age, race, sex). Such auxiliary data exist in the National Health and Nutrition Examination Survey (NHANES).

For concreteness, consider fifty-year-old non-Hispanic (NH) males whose race is either black or white. I use a standard binary classification of high blood pressure (HBP) in Go et al. (2013) to distinguish persons with or without HBP. The life tables show that mean remaining life span for fifty-year-old NH black and white males are 26.6 years and 29.7 years, respectively. The NHANES data estimate that the prevalence of HBP among fifty-year-old

NH black and white males are 0.426 and 0.334, respectively. Combining the life table and NHANES data yields these sharp bounds on mean remaining life span conditional on (age, sex, race, blood pressure):

> $18.1 \leq$ mean life years for (age 50, NH black male, not HBP) ≤ 35.4,
> $14.3 \leq$ mean life years for (age 50, NH black male, HBP) ≤ 38.5,
> $23.8 \leq$ mean life years for (age 50, NH white male, not HBP) ≤ 36.4,
> $15.6 \leq$ mean life years for (age 50, NH white male, HBP) ≤ 42.0.

These bounds are informative but rather wide, as they use no assumptions about how life span varies across persons. Tighter bounds can be obtained if the data are combined with assumptions restricting the distribution of life span conditional on the observed attributes. Strong enough assumptions point-identify mean life span, but these typically lack credibility. There is a substantial middle ground between making no assumptions and making assumptions strong enough to yield point identification.

Manski (2018a) reports tighter bounds that use *bounded-variation* assumptions, which restrict the magnitudes of risk assessments and the degree to which they vary with patient attributes, enabling clinicians to express quantitative judgments in a structured way. To illustrate, I continue with prediction of life span.

One may find it reasonable to conjecture that, holding (age, sex, race) fixed, persons with HBP have lower life expectancy than those without HBP. One may also conjecture that black males tend to face various health disadvantages relative to white males beyond high blood pressure and, hence, that black males have lower life expectancy than white males, conditional on hypertension status. Going further, one may perhaps find it credible to conjecture that, at age fifty and conditional on hypertension status, the life expectancy of white males is between zero and 2.5 years greater than black males.

Combining these assumptions with the life table and NHANES data yields these bounds on mean remaining life spans:

> $29.4 \leq$ mean life years for (age 50, NH black male, not HBP) ≤ 35.4,
> $14.7 \leq$ mean life years for (age 50, NH black male, HBP) ≤ 22.9,
> $31.9 \leq$ mean life years for (age 50, NH white male, not HBP) ≤ 36.4,
> $16.3 \leq$ mean life years for (age 50, NH white male, HBP) ≤ 25.4.

These bounds are highly informative. They reveal that the life expectancy of fifty-year-old blacks and whites without HBP is at least 6.5 years higher than that of those with HBP.

3.5. Credible Inference with Observational Data

I promised earlier to show that observational data yield quantifiable partial conclusions about treatment response even without any knowledge of the process used to allocate treatments. Moreover, tighter partial conclusions hold when the data are combined with credible assumptions. This section explains basic ideas and the remainder of the chapter elaborates.

BOUNDS WITH NO KNOWLEDGE OF COUNTERFACTUAL OUTCOMES

Manski (1990b) begins by asking what one can learn about treatment response without knowledge of the process generating counterfactual outcomes. The identification region is obtained by contemplating all logically possible values of the counterfactual outcomes. The practical findings include bounds on success probabilities and on mean and median outcomes under specified treatments. These bounds quantify what one can learn from observational data without assuming random treatment assignment or any other restriction on treatment allocation.

Suppose that the objective is to learn the success probability for a treatment with a binary outcome, or to learn the mean or median value of a continuous outcome such as life span. Lower bounds on these measures of treatment response are determined by conjecturing that all counterfactual outcomes take the smallest values that can possibly occur. Upper bounds are determined analogously.

The literature on evidence-based medicine has emphasized comparison of alternative treatments through the average treatment effect (ATE). Suppose that treatments A and B are being compared. Then the ATE is the mean outcome that would occur if all patients were to receive B minus the mean outcome that would occur if they were all to receive A. Without knowledge of counterfactual outcomes, the lower bound on the ATE equals the lower bound on the mean outcome with treatment B minus the upper bound on the mean outcome with A. The upper bound on the ATE is analogous.

Complement 3B derives the bound on success probabilities with a binary outcome, which are particularly simple. Logically, a success probability must lie between 0 and 1. The width of the bound on a treatment's success probability is the fraction of patients in the study population who do not actually receive this treatment; that is, the fraction for whom the treatment outcome is counterfactual.

When the outcome is binary, the ATE comparing treatments A and B is the success probability under B minus that under A. Complement 3B derives the bound on the ATE. The width of this bound is the sum of the fractions of the study population for whom each treatment is counterfactual. Logically, the ATE must lie between the values −1 and 1, a bound of width 2. The sum of the fractions of the study population for whom each treatment is counterfactual is necessarily less than 2. Hence, an observational study yields information about the ATE even without any knowledge of counterfactual outcomes.

The width of the bound on the ATE is particularly simple when A and B are the only feasible treatments. Then every patient in the study population receives one of the two treatments and not the other. Hence, the width of the bound on the ATE necessarily equals 1. This width is half the width of the logical bound [−1, 1] that would hold if the data from the observational study were not available. Thus, an observational study performed with no knowledge of counterfactual outcomes takes one halfway toward learning the exact value of the ATE in the study population.

SENTENCING AND RECIDIVISM

To illustrate, I will use the Manski and Nagin (1998) analysis of sentencing and recidivism of juvenile offenders in the state of Utah. Sentencing and recidivism may appear remote from patient care. However, the formal structure of this matter is analogous to patient care, with judges in the role of clinicians and juvenile offenders in the role of patients. The feasible treatments are alternative sentencing options. The outcome of interest is recidivism; that is, future offending. Beyond the formal analogy with patient care, there is also some substantive similarity. Sentencing of juvenile offenders has sometimes been viewed as an aspect of public health policy rather than criminal justice policy.

Judges in Utah have had the discretion to order various sentences for juvenile offenders. Some offenders have been given sentences with no residential confinement (treatment A) and others have been sentenced to confinement (treatment B). These are akin to surveillance and aggressive treatment.

A possible alternative policy would be to replace judicial discretion with a mandate that all offenders in Utah be confined. Another would be to mandate that no offenders be confined. To compare these alternatives, we supposed that the outcome of interest is whether an offender commits a new offense in the two-year period following sentencing. This is a binary outcome, no new offense indicating that treatment succeeds and commission of a new offense indicating that it fails. The average treatment effect is the difference between treatments A and B in their probabilities of success.

We obtained data on the sentences received and the recidivism outcomes realized by all male offenders in Utah who were born from 1970 through 1974 and who were convicted of offenses before they reached age sixteen. The Utah data reveal that 11 percent of the offenders were sentenced to confinement and that 23 percent of these persons did not offend again in the two years following sentencing. The remaining 89 percent were sentenced to non-confinement and 41 percent of these persons did not offend again.

If one were to assume that judges randomly sentence offenders to the two treatments, the observed outcome data would imply that the success probability for confinement is 0.23 and for non-confinement is 0.41. Hence, the ATE would be −0.18, indicating that non-confinement is superior to confinement. However, one may object that it is not credible to assume that judges sentence randomly. This motivates the analysis in Manski and Nagin (1998).

We compute bounds that assume no knowledge of counterfactual outcomes, using the results in complement 3B. The lower bound on the success probability for treatment B is 0.03 and the upper bound is 0.92. The bound has width 0.89 because 0.89 of the offenders in the study population were not confined. We do not know what the recidivism of these persons would have been if they had been confined. Analogously, the lower bound on the success probability for treatment A is 0.36 and the upper bound is 0.47, a bound of width 0.11. Thus, the data reveal much more about recidivism with mandatory non-confinement than with mandatory confinement. The bound on the ATE is [−0.44, 0.56], whose width is 1 as explained above.

ASSUMPTIONS USING INSTRUMENTAL VARIABLES

Assuming nothing about counterfactual outcomes provides a logical starting point for research on treatment response. Yet researchers understandably would like to draw stronger conclusions than those implied by observational data alone. For most of the twentieth century, econometric research brought to bear assumptions that are strong enough to point-identify average treatment effects and other features of treatment response. But the cost in credibility was high.

Modern research on partial identification explores the vast middle ground between making no assumptions and ones that yield point identification.

The goal is to illuminate the tradeoff alluded to in the Law of Decreasing Credibility: Stronger assumptions yield conclusions that are more powerful but less credible. Manski (2007a, chs. 7 and 9) describes findings on the identifying power of a spectrum of middle-ground assumptions, some placing restrictions on the process of treatment allocation and some on the outcomes yielded by alternative treatments.

An especially fertile subject of study has been the identifying power of assumptions that use an *instrumental variable* (IV). An IV is an observable covariate whose value varies across a study population. The term instrumental variable originates with Reiersol (1945), who thought of such a covariate as an instrument or tool that may help to identify an object of interest. Reiersol and other econometricians of his time used IVs in combination with other assumptions to point-identify linear structural equation systems. See Goldberger (1972) for an informative review of the classical literature.

Modern econometric research uses IVs to help address many identification problems, including identification of treatment response. Whatever the application may be, it is important to understand that observation of an IV does not per se carry any implications for inference. It is useful only when combined with an assumption that has identifying power. Empirical researchers often ask whether some covariate is or is not a "valid instrument" in an application of interest. The expression "valid instrument" is imprecise because it focuses attention on the covariate used as the IV, without reference to the accompanying assumption. It would be more precise to ask whether an assumption using an instrumental variable is credible.

A particularly simple assumption using an IV supposes that different subpopulations of a study population share the same distribution of treatment response (or at least the same mean response), but experienced different processes of treatment allocation. For example, the Manski and Nagin (1998) study of sentencing and recidivism entertained the assumption that offenders who reside in different judicial districts of Utah respond to sentencing similarly but faced different sentencing selection rules. In this case, the IV is an indicator variable denoting the judicial district in which an offender lives.

When studying patient care, one might similarly assume that patient subpopulations treated by different groups of clinicians have the same distribution of treatment response, or at least the same mean response. This assumption may be credible in some studies of geographic variation in clinical practice. Then the IV is the geographic area in which a patient is treated.

For example, when examining variation in hospital re-admissions rates between hospitals in Boston and New Haven, Fisher et al. (1994) discussed reasons why they believed the patient populations in the two cities are similar. The assumption of geographic invariance in the distribution of treatment response is maintained regularly in analyses of multicenter trials that combine data on patient outcomes across multiple treatment centers. These analyses typically assume that patients treated in different centers respond to treatment in the same way.

Whatever the application may be, an assumption that different subpopulations of a study population share the same distribution of treatment response (or the same mean response) generates what is now called an *intersection bound* on treatment response. The basic idea is straightforward. Consideration of each subpopulation separately yields a bound that uses no knowledge of treatment allocation, as described above. The assumption of a common distribution of treatment response across subpopulations implies that the common distribution must simultaneously lie in each of these no-assumptions bounds. In other words, it must lie in the intersection of the bounds. The same reasoning applies if one assumes only the same mean response across subpopulations.

Computation of intersection bounds is simple if one assumes only that mean treatment response is common across subpopulations; see Manski (1990b, 2007a). Then the lower bound is the maximum of the lower bounds obtained using no assumptions and the upper bound is the minimum of the upper bounds obtained this way. Computation is more complex if one assumes that the entire distribution of treatment response is common across subpopulations; see Balke and Pearl (1997), Manski (2003), and Kitagawa (2009).

CASE STUDY: BOUNDING THE MORTALITY EFFECTS OF SWAN-GANZ CATHETERIZATION

The Swan-Ganz catheter is a sensory device placed in an artery of cardiac patients in the intensive care unit (ICU), the aim being to guide therapy. Catheterization has been a standard practice since the 1970s. However, a series of observational studies from the 1980s onward have reported that its use increases patient mortality; Fowler and Cook (2003) summarize the history. A particularly influential study by Connors et al. (1996) examined data on mortality outcomes among a population of patients admitted to the ICU and concluded that patients who receive Swan-Ganz catheterization during their first day in the ICU are more likely to die a week or a half year after their admission.

To point-identify treatment response, Connors et al. (1996) assumed that patients are assigned randomly to catheterization or non-catheterization, conditional on certain patient attributes. The credibility of this assumption is questionable. Clinicians in the ICU select which patients do and do not receive catheterization. Clinicians may base their decisions on mortality-relevant patient attributes that they observe but that were not considered in the Connors et al. study.

With this concern in mind, Bhattacharya, Shaikh, and Vytlacil (2012) re-analyze the Connors et al. data, using an IV and other assumptions to bound the effect of Swan-Ganz catheterization on mortality outcomes. Their analysis permits the possibility of differences across patients who do and do not receive catheterization.

The authors use a period during the week (weekday vs. weekend) as an instrument for administration of catheterization. They observe that clinician propensity to catheterize patients varies during the week, with catheterization occurring less frequently on weekends. They assume that mean treatment response is the same for patients admitted to the ICU on a weekday or during the weekend. Applying the identification analysis of Manski (1990b), they find that the IV assumption yields an informative bound on the average effect of catheterization on mortality. However, the bound is not narrow enough to reveal the sign of the average effect.

To achieve a tighter bound, the authors assume a nonparametric selection model that jointly explains clinician choice of treatment and patient mortality. Combining the IV assumption with the selection model, they find that catheterization increases mortality at thirty days after catheterization and beyond.

This article is a carefully executed application of partial identification analysis to a prominent medical problem of treatment response. The empirical work makes clear how imposition of additional assumptions tightens the bounds obtained. The authors provide a thoughtful discussion of why they find credible the instrument that they apply.

3.6. Identification of Response to Testing and Treatment

I have thus far discussed analysis of treatment response with specified knowledge of patient attributes. A common prelude to treatment choice is to learn more about a patient. This section considers a common scenario in which a patient presents to a clinician, who initially observes some attributes such as demographic traits and medical history. The clinician may choose a treatment immediately, or he may first order a medical procedure that yields further information about the patient's health status. Clinicians use the term *screening* when ordering informative procedures for unsymptomatic patients. They use the term *diagnostic testing* when considering symptomatic patients. I will use the term *testing* to cover both.

The clinical decision has several aspects. Should the test be ordered? What treatment should be chosen in the absence of the test? What treatment should be chosen when the test is performed, and the result observed?

OPTIMAL TESTING AND TREATMENT

Phelps and Mushlin (1988) initiated study of this sequential decision problem using the rational-expectations optimization framework described in chapter 1. The value of performing a test is that doing so reveals a patient attribute that the clinician would not observe otherwise, namely the test result. The potential usefulness of testing is expressed by the *expected value of information*, defined succinctly by Meltzer (2001, p. 119) as: "the change in expected utility with the collection of information."

It can be shown that the expected value of information is necessarily non-negative and is positive if the result affects the optimal treatment. It follows that a clinician should always order a test if performing the test has no direct negative effect on patient utility. However, performing a test may negatively affect utility. For example, biopsies, scans, and colonoscopies are invasive and expensive procedures. Hence, a test should be performed only if the expected value of information outweighs the direct utility cost.

Phelps and Mushlin assumed that clinicians have the knowledge required to optimize testing and treatment. This includes knowledge of (a) expected patient utility with each treatment, in the absence of testing; (b) the probability distribution for the test result; and (c) expected patient utility with each treatment, with knowledge of the test result. They characterized optimal testing and treatment given this knowledge.

Optimal testing and treatment is a subtle problem when the test result is informative about patient health status but not definitive. Often a test has two possible results, positive or negative. Clinicians call a test result "positive" if it suggests illness and "negative" otherwise. A result is said to be a "false positive" if it suggests illness, but the patient is not actually ill. It is said to be a "false negative" if it suggests no illness, but the patient is ill. Determination of optimal testing and treatment requires knowledge of the probabilities with which a test yields false positive and negative results. Phelps and Mushlin assume that clinicians have this knowledge.

IDENTIFICATION OF TESTING AND TREATMENT RESPONSE WITH OBSERVATIONAL DATA

The analysis of Phelps and Mushlin is instructive, providing a clear prescription for optimal patient care when clinicians have the requisite knowledge of testing and treatment response. In principle, one might obtain this knowledge by performing an ideal randomized trial. A trial with multiple arms, one for each possible testing and treatment decision, could yield the knowledge of test results and treatment response needed to optimize. However, performance of this ideal trial is rare. Often the only available evidence is observational data generated by the testing and treatment decisions that occur in clinical practice. Then it may be unrealistic to suppose that clinicians have the knowledge that Phelps and Mushlin assumed.

Manski (2013b) characterizes the partial knowledge obtained when one combines observational data on a study population with various assumptions that restrict counterfactual testing results and treatment outcomes. I consider the common setting where the test has two possible results, positive or negative. I suppose that there are two feasible treatments, A being surveillance and B being aggressive treatment.

A common clinical practice is to choose aggressive treatment if and only if a test is performed and the result is positive. The chosen treatment is surveillance if the test result is negative or if the patient is not tested. I call this practice *aggressive treatment with positive testing* (ATPT). Clinicians sometimes use the term "over-diagnosis" to describe treatment resulting from a false positive test result. I study identification when the available evidence is observation of a study population that adheres to the ATPT practice.

In this setting, an observational study reveals some but not all the knowledge needed to optimize patient care for a group of patients who share the same initial attributes. One can observe test results for patients who are tested. One can observe health outcomes under (i) treatment A for patients who are not tested, (ii) treatment A for patients who are tested and have a negative test result, and (iii) treatment B for patients who are tested and have a positive test result.

Other outcomes are counterfactual. One does not observe test results for patients who are not tested. One does not observe health outcomes under (i) treatment B for patients who are not tested, (ii) treatment B for patients who are tested and have a negative test result, and (iii) treatment A for patients who are tested and have a positive test result. These health outcomes are counterfactual because the ATPT practice assigns treatment B if and only if a patient is tested and has a positive test result.

Manski (2013b) shows that the observational evidence yields informative bounds on some of the quantities that determine optimal patient care. I initially derive bounds without making assumptions that restrict counterfactual testing and treatment outcomes. I then show what more can be learned if the evidence is combined with assumptions that may be credible in some settings.

One potentially credible assumption uses the test result as a *monotone instrumental variable*, as defined in Manski and Pepper (2000). Patients with negative test results are often thought to be healthier than ones with positive results. Hence, a clinician may find it credible to predict that patients with negative test results have better future prospects, on average, than do patients with positive results. Consider, for example, use of a PET or CT scan to detect metastasis of a cancer diagnosed at a primary site. A clinician may reasonably predict better prospects, on average, for patients with negative scans than for those with positive ones. Formally, this makes the test result a monotone instrumental variable, which has identifying power.

Another potentially credible assumption may be that testing cannot directly improve welfare but may decrease it. This assumption is realistic in the common setting where testing has no therapeutic effect but is invasive or costly. Formally, this is a version of the assumption of *monotone treatment response* studied in Manski (1997). It also has identifying power.

The two assumptions posed here may be used in conjunction with one another. Doing so further tightens the bounds using the data alone.

MEASURING THE ACCURACY OF DIAGNOSTIC TESTS

The above discussion of identification with data from ATPT practice observes that such data only partially reveal the health outcomes of patients who are tested. This may seem at odds with the medical literature on accuracy of diagnostic tests, which regularly reports point measures of test accuracy, known as *sensitivity* and *specificity*. Unfortunately, sensitivity and specificity do not provide the information that a clinician would want to have to inform patient care.

A clinician who orders a diagnostic test as a prelude to treatment wants to use the test result to assess the patient's risk of illness. That is, the clinician wants to know the probability that the patient is ill conditional on observed patient attributes and on the test result. Statistics on the sensitivity and specificity of a test do not reveal this probability.

The sensitivity and specificity of a test are defined to be the probabilities that a test yields a "true positive" or a "true negative" result, respectively. That is, sensitivity is the probability that the test result is positive conditional on the patient being ill. Specificity is the probability that the result is negative conditional on the patient being healthy. These probabilities permit one to predict the test result conditional on patient health status. However, the clinician's problem is to predict the patient's health status conditional on the test result.

Perceptive writers on diagnostic testing have long cautioned that sensitivity and specificity do not inform patient risk assessment. For example, Altman and Bland (1994) wrote:

> The whole point of a diagnostic test is to use it to make a diagnosis, so we need to know the probability that the test will give the correct diagnosis. The sensitivity and specificity do not give us this information. Instead we must approach the data from the direction of the test results, using predictive values. Positive predictive value is the proportion of patients with positive test results who are correctly diagnosed. Negative predictive value is the proportion of patients with negative test results who are correctly diagnosed. (p. 102)

Despite the cautions expressed by writers such as Altman and Bland, it remains standard to measure the accuracy of diagnostic tests by their sensitivity and specificity.

3.7. Prediction Combining Multiple Studies

In chapter 2, I cautioned against use of meta-analysis to combine the point predictions of disparate studies. Dismissing meta-analysis leaves open how one might credibly combine multiple studies.

Suppose that one obtains N precise probabilistic predictions of a health outcome. Suppose that each prediction uses informative data and a plausible prediction model, but the predictions disagree with one another. It may be that one is accurate or that none are accurate. There is no logical reason to form a simple or weighted average of the predictions, as has been recommended by advocates of meta-analysis such as DerSimonian and Laird (1986). One can only conclude that the predictions pose N possible futures, with others perhaps possible as well.

Explicit statement of this conclusion is rare in the medical literature, but there are some notable cases. I use breast cancer risk assessment to demonstrate.

COMBINING MULTIPLE BREAST CANCER RISK ASSESSMENTS

The Gail Model discussed in chapter 1 is perhaps the most prominent model that predicts future development of breast cancer in women with specified personal attributes. However, it is not the only such model. The review article of Amir et al. (2010) considers five other models as well: the Claus Model, the BRCAPRO Model, the Jonker Model, the IBIS Model, and the BOADICEA Model.

These five studies differ from one another in multiple respects, including the patient attributes used to condition predictions, the mathematical forms of the models, and the observational data used to estimate model parameters. As a result, they often yield different probabilistic predictions when applied to women with specified attributes. Domchek et al. (2003) compare the Gail and Claus Models and find that: "Concordance of the two models is only fair, with the greatest discrepancies seen with nulliparity, multiple benign breast biopsies, and a strong paternal or first-degree family history" (p. 597).

When multiple studies yield disparate precise probabilistic predictions, uncertainty becomes inevitable. A clinician who insists on making a precise probabilistic prediction must choose among those that are available. Amir et al. (2010) attempt to assist such a clinician by presenting a flowchart (their figure 3) that recommends how a clinician should choose among the five models that the authors compare. The recommended choice depends on certain patient attributes. The authors note: "It is clear that some models are better than others in certain circumstances" (p. 687).

Other writers do not agree with the attempt by Amir et al. to provide a guideline for clinicians to choose among the models. In an editorial commenting on the Amir et al. article, Gail and Mai (2010) comment:

> In our opinion, the flowchart in figure 3 of Amir et al. should only be regarded as a preliminary attempt to synthesize a complex literature and should not be used as a true guide to action. In fact, the lack of independent assessments of calibration of these models . . . is a serious deficiency in the confirmatory research needed to show that these models yield reliable risk estimates. (p. 666)

I am aware of two articles that approach combination of predictions in a manner that I think more appropriate. In their review article comparing the Gail and Claus Models, Domchek et al. (2003) reject the notion that a clinician must choose one or the other model. Instead, they suggest that the two models "may provide helpful ranges" of probabilistic predictions (p. 600).

Mandelblatt et al. (2009) report on an ambitious project that uses multiple models to generate a range of hypothetical predictions of breast cancer development and mortality under alternative strategies for mammography screening. They state:

> Each model has a different structure and assumptions and some varying input variables, so no single method can be used to validate results against an external gold standard. . . . Overall, using 6 models to project a range of plausible screening outcomes provides implicit cross-validation, with the range of results from the models as a measure of uncertainty. (p. 740)

COMBINING PARTIAL PREDICTIONS

Domchek et al. (2003) and Mandelblatt et al. (2009) appropriately recognized that, when multiple plausible models generate a range of predictions, the correct prediction is uncertain. They suggested using the range of results to quantify the uncertainty. This suggestion is more sensible than averaging the predictions, which suppresses uncertainty. However, it does not go far enough.

The observed range of results only measures the variation in predictions across studies that have been reported in the literature. It does not measure the potential variation that would be obtained using all plausible models. Thus, the observed range of results understates actual uncertainty. In the language of partial identification analysis, the observed range of results is a subset of the identification region for the prediction of interest.

Manski (2019b) observes that, if medical research were performed with explicit recognition of identification problems, it would combine multiple studies in a different way. One would first specify a prediction of interest—designating the relevant patient population, the presumed features of patient care, and the outcome to be predicted. One would next determine what each existing study credibly reveals, as quantified by the bound it yields for the prediction of interest.

This done, one would combine the findings of the existing studies by computing the intersection of the bounds that they yield. This intersection expresses the conclusion that one can logically draw, because the prediction of interest must simultaneously lie in the bound obtained with each study. One would thus compute an intersection bound, using the studies as an instrumental variable.

A benefit of performing research in this manner is that it would resolve a long-standing open question in evidence-based medical research: How should one combine the findings of observational studies and trials? Jointly considering internal and external validity, an observational study and a trial may each partially identify a prediction of interest. The truth must lie in the intersection of the bounds obtained with each type of data.

4

Reasonable Care under Uncertainty

Chapter 1 cited psychological research which concludes that clinicians exercise imperfect judgment. Chapter 2 called attention to questionable methodological practices in evidence-based medical research. Chapter 3 showed that combining evidence from trials or observational studies with credible assumptions seldom yields precise probabilistic predictions of patient outcomes conditional on observed attributes, but it may yield informative bounds.

Given all of this, I conclude that clinicians and guideline developers should view patient care as a problem of decision making under uncertainty. The remainder of the book explores the implications.

4.1. Qualitative Recognition of Uncertainty

Qualitative recognition of uncertainty has been common in medical decision making. Considering treatment of cancer, Mullins, Montgomery, and Tunis (2010, p. 59) observe that: "there is considerable uncertainty surrounding the clinical benefits and harms associated with oncology treatments." Institute of Medicine (2011, p. 33) calls attention to the assertion by the Evidence-Based Medicine Working Group that: "clinicians must accept uncertainty and the notion that clinical decisions are often made with scant knowledge of their true impact."

The GRADE system classifies quality of evidence this way (Guyatt et al., 2008, p. 926):

> High quality—Further research is very unlikely to change our confidence in the estimate of effect.
>
> Moderate quality—Further research is likely to have an important impact on our confidence in the estimate of effect and may change the estimate.
>
> Low quality—Further research is very likely to have an important impact on our confidence in the estimate of effect and is likely to change the estimate.
>
> Very low quality—Any estimate of effect is very uncertain.

In general, this classification calls on researchers to assess quality of evidence on a case-by-case basis. However, the GRADE authors provide specific recommendations for rating the relative quality of trial and observational data. Expressing the conventional perspective that internal validity is more important than external validity, they write:

> Evidence based on randomised controlled trials begins as high quality evidence, but our confidence in the evidence may be decreased for several reasons. . . . Although observational studies . . . start with a "low quality" rating, grading upwards may be warranted if the magnitude of the treatment effect is very large . . . , if there is evidence of a dose-response relation or if all plausible biases would decrease the magnitude of an apparent treatment effect. (p. 926)

Some CPGs use a rating system to rank the strength of their treatment recommendations by the certainty that they are correct. For example, the James et al. article summarizing guidelines for treatment of hypertension describes its rating system this way (2014, p. 510):

> A Strong Recommendation . . . There is high certainty based on evidence that the net benefit is substantial.
>
> B Moderate Recommendation . . . There is moderate certainty based on evidence that the net benefit is moderate to substantial or there is high certainty that the net benefit is moderate.
>
> C Weak Recommendation . . . There is at least moderate certainty based on evidence that there is a small net benefit.

D Recommendation against . . . There is at least moderate certainty based on evidence that it has no net benefit or that risks/harms outweigh benefits.

E Expert Opinion . . . Net benefit is unclear. Balance of benefits and harms cannot be determined because of no evidence, insufficient evidence, unclear evidence, or conflicting evidence, but the committee thought it was important to provide clinical guidance and make a recommendation. Further research is recommended in this area.

N No Recommendation for or against . . . Net benefit is unclear. Balance of benefits and harms cannot be determined because of no evidence, insufficient evidence, unclear evidence, or conflicting evidence, and the committee thought no recommendation should be made. Further research is recommended in this area.

Perhaps the most compelling evidence that guideline developers recognize uncertainty qualitatively is that CPGs regularly change their recommendations as new research accumulates. For example, complement 1A describes how a sequence of randomized trials over the past twenty years have improved knowledge regarding the usefulness of sentinel lymph node biopsy as a diagnostic test and completion lymph node dissection as an adjuvant treatment for potential visceral metastasis of melanoma. As a result, guidelines regarding these procedures have changed in the past and continue to evolve.

4.2. Formalizing Uncertainty

Curiously, qualitative recognition of uncertainty has not led guideline developers to examine patient care formally as a problem of decision making under uncertainty. The influential Institute of Medicine (2011) report on guideline development repeatedly called for the development of *rigorous* CPGs. Yet the eight standards proposed by the IOM committee (pp. 6–9) are uncomfortably vague.

Although the IOM report aimed to inform medical decision making, it brought to bear no formal decision analysis. It discussed decision analysis only briefly and expressed skepticism about formal decision analysis, stating:

A frontier of evidence-based medicine is decision analytic modeling in health care alternatives' assessment. . . . Although the field is currently fraught with controversy, the committee acknowledges it as exciting and potentially promising, however, decided the state of the art is not ready for direct comment. (2011, p. 171)

The report did not explain the basis for this assessment.

I find the IOM perspective surprising. Medical research makes much use of sophisticated biological science and technology. Why then has guideline development remained informal and qualitative?

The foundations of analysis of decisions under uncertainty were largely in place by the middle of the twentieth century and applications in many domains have since become common. Applications within medicine have been promoted since the 1980s by the Society for Medical Decision Making. In 1984, David Eddy, a prominent early developer of guidelines, wrote:

people who want to promote policies regarding the use of medical procedures can learn the necessary languages. Over the past few hundred years languages have been developed for collecting and interpreting evidence (statistics), dealing with uncertainty (probability theory), synthesizing evidence and estimating outcomes (mathematics), and making decisions (economics and decision theory.) These languages are not currently learned by most clinical policymakers; they should be. (p.87)

Yet as recently as 2011, the IOM report referred to decision analysis as "a frontier of evidence-based medicine" in which "the state of the art is not ready for direct comment."

Formal analysis of patient care under uncertainty has much to contribute to guideline development and to clinical decision making. This chapter explains. To begin, I explain how decision theorists formalize uncertainty.

STATES OF NATURE

The standard formalization of decision under uncertainty supposes that a decision maker must choose among a set of feasible actions. Our concern is patient care when the decision maker is a clinician or a guideline developer. The actions are the feasible alternative treatments for a patient. They may, for example, be surveillance or aggressive treatment.

A decision maker faces uncertainty if the welfare achieved by an action depends on the *state of nature*; that is, on features of the environment that are incompletely known. The starting point for decision theory is to suppose that the decision maker lists all the states of nature that he believes could possibly occur. This list, called the *state space*, expresses partial knowledge. The larger the state space, the less the decision maker knows about the consequences of each action.

In patient care, the state of nature may encompass a patient's current health status, how the disease will progress in this patient, and the patient's response to alternative treatments. Consider, for example, a clinician who has performed a prostate exam on a male patient and obtained the result of a PSA test. The exam and test results may be informative about the risk of prostate cancer. However, the clinician may not know whether the patient has developed cancer, how rapidly the disease would metastasize in this patient in the absence of aggressive treatment, or the side effects the patient would experience with alternative treatments.

When considering patient outcomes, one may find it useful to define states of nature in deterministic personal terms or in distributional group terms. A personal state of nature is a patient-specific outcome. A group state is the distribution of outcomes for patients with specified observed attributes.

To illustrate the distinction, consider the presence or absence of illness. A personal state would indicate whether a specified patient is ill. A group state would indicate the fraction of patients with specified observed attributes who are ill. Or consider life span with a certain treatment. A personal state would indicate a specific patient's life span if treated in a given manner. A group state would indicate the distribution of life spans for patients with specified observed attributes if they were all treated in this manner.

4.3. Optimal and Reasonable Decisions

The fundamental difficulty of decision making under uncertainty is clear even in a simple setting with two feasible actions and two states of nature. Suppose that one action yields higher welfare in one state of nature and the other action yields higher welfare in the other state. Then the decision maker does not know which action is better. Thus, optimization is impossible.

Suppose that the two feasible actions are surveillance and aggressive treatment. A personal state of nature may be the presence or absence of disease. As discussed earlier, it is common for surveillance to yield higher welfare in the absence of disease and for aggressive treatment to be better in the presence of disease. If so, a clinician who does not know whether disease is present or absent cannot determine whether surveillance or aggressive treatment is optimal.

At the outset of chapter 1, I quoted from the Institute of Medicine (2011, p. 4): "Clinical practice guidelines are statements that include recommendations intended to optimize patient care." The IOM Committee did not explain what it meant by "optimize." It specifically did not address formation of guidelines for patient care under uncertainty.

Decision theory suggests a two-step process when facing uncertainty, the first step being obvious and the second being subtle. The first step is to eliminate *dominated* actions; that is, those which are surely inferior to others. Formally, an action is dominated if some other action is at least as good in all states of nature and superior in some state. The second step is to choose among the actions that are not dominated. This is subtle because there is no optimal way to choose among undominated alternatives. There are only various reasonable ways, each with its own properties.

The term "reasonable" inevitably has multiple interpretations. In a monograph on statistical decision theory, Ferguson (1967) explained:

> It is a natural reaction to search for a "best" decision rule, a rule that has the smallest risk no matter what the true state of nature. Unfortunately, *situations in which a best decision rule exists are rare and uninteresting.* For each fixed state of nature there may be a best action for the statistician to take. However, this best action will differ, in general, for different states of nature, so that no one action can be presumed best over all. (p. 28)

He went on to write: "A *reasonable* rule is one that is better than just guessing" (p. 29).

Once one accepts that there are multiple reasonable ways to make decisions under uncertainty, the admonition of the medical literature that clinicians should adhere to CPGs loses some of its force. I noted in chapter 1 that commentaries often exhort clinicians to adhere to CPGs to reduce "unnecessary" or "unwarranted" variation in clinical practice. This prescription for clinical practice is justified when medical knowledge suffices to distinguish optimal treatments from dominated ones. It is not justified when clinicians must choose among alternative undominated treatments. Then different reasonable criteria for decision making may yield different treatment choices. The next section explains.

4.4. Reasonable Decision Criteria

What are reasonable ways to choose among undominated actions? When addressing this question, decision theorists have distinguished three primary situations regarding information that a decision maker may or may not have beyond specification of the state space. They have studied decision criteria suited to each situation.

DECISIONS WITH RATIONAL EXPECTATIONS

In the situation with the strongest information, the decision maker asserts knowledge of an objective probabilistic process generating observed outcomes. I discussed this situation in chapter 1, using the economic term *rational expectations* as shorthand. The supposition was that a clinician knows the actual distribution of health outcomes that may potentially occur if a group of patients with specified observed attributes are treated in a certain manner.

When the objective is to maximize a social welfare function that sums up the benefits and costs of treatment across the group of patients, I observed that a clinician with rational expectations has sufficient knowledge to optimize patient care. It is optimal to give each patient in the group the treatment that maximizes the mean outcome within the group.

MAXIMIZATION OF SUBJECTIVE EXPECTED UTILITY

In the intermediate situation, the decision maker does not assert knowledge of an objective probabilistic process generating outcomes. Instead he introspects and places a subjective probability distribution on outcomes. Decision theorists often refer to such a decision maker as a *Bayesian*, associating subjective probability with suggestions made in the 1700s by Reverend Thomas Bayes.

Recall our discussion of subjective clinical judgment in chapter 1. A clinician wants to predict an outcome for a patient under treatment but lacks an evidence-based basis for prediction. To exercise judgment, the clinician might place a subjective distribution on the patient's outcomes.

The usual prescription for decision making with a subjective distribution is to maximize subjective expected utility. The potential problem, of course, is that the asserted subjective distribution may not accurately describe the actual process generating patient outcomes. Hence, maximizing subjective expected utility may not optimize patient care.

DECISIONS UNDER AMBIGUITY: THE MAXIMIN
AND MINIMAX-REGRET CRITERIA

In the situation with the weakest information, the decision maker asserts no knowledge beyond that the true state of nature lies within the specified state space. Decision theorists refer to this as a situation of *ambiguity* or *deep uncertainty*.

A clinician may conceptualize ambiguity in terms of personal or group states of nature. Consider prediction of life span. In personal terms, the clinician may know that if a specific patient were treated in a certain manner, life span would be between 2 months and 5 years. In group terms, the clinician may know that if a group of patients with specified observed attributes were all treated in this manner, the mean life span of patients in the group would be between 6 months and 3 years. The clinician may also be able to bound other features of the life span distribution, such as median life span and the fraction of patients who survive more than one year.

The identification problems studied in chapter 3 generate problems of patient care under ambiguity, conceptualized in terms of group states of nature. In each setting considered there, one wants to learn the distribution of outcomes for patients with specified observed attributes. Combining the available data with credible assumptions, one concludes that the outcome distribution lies in the set of distributions called its identification region. Thus, the identification region for an outcome distribution is its state space.

When making a choice under ambiguity, a reasonable way to act is to use a decision criterion that achieves adequate performance in all states of nature. There are multiple ways to formalize this idea. The two most commonly studied are the maximin and minimax-regret (MR) criteria.

Maximin Decisions

The maximin criterion chooses an action that maximizes the minimum welfare that might possibly occur across all states of nature. Thus, a clinician using the maximin criterion makes a worst-case prediction for the outcome of each treatment. The clinician then chooses the treatment with the least-bad worse-case prediction.

The idea of a worst-case prediction may be conceptualized in either personal or group terms. I illustrate the former here and the latter in section 4.5. Let life span be the outcome of interest. A clinician using the maximin criterion would choose the treatment that yields the largest value for minimal life span. Suppose that treatment A is known to yield a patient-specific life span between 2 months and 5 years, while treatment B yields a patient-specific life span between 4 months and 3 years. Then the clinician chooses treatment B because its minimal life span (4 months) is longer than that of treatment A (2 months).

Minimax-Regret Decisions

The minimax-regret criterion considers each state of nature and computes the loss in welfare that would occur if one were to choose a specified action rather than the one that is best in this state. This quantity, called *regret*, measures the nearness to optimality of the specified action in the state of nature.

The decision maker must choose without knowing the true state. To achieve adequate performance in all states of nature, he computes the maximum regret of each action; that is, the maximum distance from optimality that the action would yield across all states. The MR criterion chooses an action that minimizes this maximum distance from optimality.

To illustrate, consider further the illustration with two treatments and life span as the outcome of interest. Suppose that patient response to treatments A and B is known to vary genetically with the presence or absence of a specific mutation. Treatment A yields life span 5 years if a patient has the mutation and 2 months without the mutation. Treatment B yields life span 4 months if a patient has the mutation and 3 years without the mutation.

In this setting there are two personal states of nature, indicating presence or absence of the mutation. A clinician using the minimax-regret criterion would observe that A is the optimal treatment if the patient has the mutation and B is optimal in the absence of the mutation. In the state of nature with the mutation, regret under treatment A is zero and regret under treatment B is 4.67 years; that is, 5 years minus 4 months. In the state of nature without the mutation, regret under treatment B is zero and regret under treatment A is 2.83 years; that is, 3 years minus 2 months. Hence, maximum regret is 2.83 years for treatment A and 4.67 years for B. Thus, treatment A minimizes maximum regret.

Discussion

The maximin and MR criteria are sometimes confused with one another. The life span illustration demonstrates that they differ, with treatment B solving the maximin problem and A solving the minimax-regret problem. Whereas the maximin criterion considers only the worst outcome that an action may yield, MR considers the worst outcome relative to what is achievable in a given state of nature.

Savage (1951), who introduced the idea of minimax regret, distinguished it sharply from maximin. He wrote that the maximin criterion is "ultrapessimistic," while minimax regret is not. Maximum regret quantifies how uncertainty—lack of knowledge of the true state of nature—potentially diminishes the quality of decisions.

It is important to understand that use of the maximin or the MR criteria does not eliminate all subjectivity in decision making. Decision theory begins with specification of a welfare function and a state space, both of which are subjective. Maximization of subjective expected utility goes a step further by placing a subjective distribution on the state space. The maximin and MR criteria do not embrace this further element of subjectivity, but they still require the decision maker to specify a welfare function and state space.

4.5. Reasonable Choice between Surveillance and Aggressive Treatment

To illustrate further the properties of alternative reasonable decision criteria, this section continues the discussion of choice between surveillance and aggressive treatment. Chapter 1 considered optimal patient care when aggressive treatment prevents the occurrence of disease or reduces the severity of disease. In both cases, it was shown that aggressive treatment is the better option if the risk of disease exceeds a computable patient-specific threshold and surveillance is the better option otherwise.

Now consider decision making when a clinician does not know a patient's precise risk of disease but can bound it. Formally, a patient is described by his observed attributes and risk of disease is the fraction of patients in this attribute group who would become ill if treated in a specified manner. Thus, risk of disease is a group state of nature whose identification region is described by a bound.

Knowledge of a bound on the risk of disease suffices to determine that surveillance is optimal if the upper bound is less than the patient-specific threshold. Similarly, aggressive treatment is optimal if the lower bound on risk of disease is greater than the threshold. Knowledge of the bound does not determine the optimal treatment if the threshold lies within the bound.

Consider, for example, risk of breast cancer. As discussed in chapter 1, an NCCN guideline calls for aggressive treatment if a woman's probability of developing the disease in the next five years exceeds 0.017. As discussed in chapter 3, a clinician who observes patient attributes beyond those used in the BCRA Tool may not know the patient's risk of cancer conditional on her observed attributes but may be able to bound the risk. Surveillance is optimal if the upper bound is less than 0.017 and aggressive treatment is optimal if the lower bound is greater than 0.017. The optimal treatment is not known if the value 0.017 lies within the bound.

When the optimal treatment is unknown, treatment choice depends on the criterion used. Complement 4A compares decision making using the subjective expected utility, maximin, and minimax-regret criteria. The structure of the choice problem is such that all three criteria yield simple solutions. In each case one acts as if the unknown risk of disease takes a specific value, whose magnitude depends on the criterion.

A clinician maximizing subjective expected utility forms a subjective mean for the patient's unknown risk of disease and acts as if the true risk equals the subjective mean. A clinician making a maximin decision acts as if the true risk of disease equals the known upper bound on risk. One making a minimax-regret decision acts as if the true risk equals the midpoint of the known bound on risk.

Thus, the maximin criterion always chooses aggressive treatment when the optimal treatment is unknown. The subjective expected utility and minimax-regret criteria may choose surveillance or aggressive treatment, depending on the specifics of the case.

4.6. Uncertainty about Patient Welfare

The discussion of uncertainty in this chapter and throughout the book focuses on uncertainty regarding patient health status and treatment response. I presume that clinicians know how patients perceive their welfare and, hence, can act with their interests in mind. Clinicians may, in principle, learn patient preferences through face-to-face discussions. Or they may administer surveys that aim to elicit preference information in more formal ways, such as by presentation of hypothetical choice exercises. See, for example, Basu and Meltzer (2007).

In practice, clinicians may nevertheless have incomplete knowledge of patient welfare. When this is the case, the decision-theoretic principles described in this chapter continue to be applicable. As a formal matter, one may expand the state space to encompass the unknown aspects of patient welfare and then proceed as explained in section 4.4.

Unfortunately, prevailing procedures for guideline development do not explicitly recognize that patients may have heterogeneous preferences. According to Basu and Meltzer (2007):

> Cost-effectiveness analysis traditionally focuses on identifying when treatments are cost-effective based on their average benefits and costs in the population. However, there may be considerable value in identifying when treatments are cost-effective for individual patients given their preferences or other personal attributes. (p. 112)

They argue that learning patient preferences would improve care. To measure the magnitude of the potential improvement, they recommend calculation of

> the expected value of individualized care (EVIC), which represents the potential value of providing physicians information on the preferences of individual patients, such as quality-of-life (QOL) weights, so as to make individualized treatment decisions. (p. 122)

The EVIC is a version of the expected value of information discussed in chapter 3 in the context of medical testing. Learning about patient preferences provides treatment-relevant information akin to learning the result of a test.

Unfortunately, prevailing practices in guideline development largely abstract from heterogeneity in patient welfare. Consider the common situation where a treatment has multiple outcomes and where patients may vary in the weight they place on each outcome. A guideline development process could recommend discovery of patient preferences, as do Basu and Meltzer. Or it could use decision-theoretic principles to make recommendations in the absence of this knowledge. Instead, guidelines commonly make omnibus recommendations intended to apply to all patients with specified health status.

The procedure for assessing multiple outcomes advocated by the GRADE system is illustrative. Guyatt et al. (2011) write:

> Guideline developers must . . . specify all potential patient-important outcomes as the first step in their endeavor. Those using GRADE for guideline development will also make a preliminary classification of outcomes into those that are critical, those that are important but not critical, and those of limited importance. The first two classes of evidence will bear on guideline recommendations; the third may or may not. Guideline

developers may choose to rate outcomes numerically on a 1–9 scale (7–9, critical; 4–6, important; and 1–3, of limited importance) to distinguish between importance categories. (p. 397)

The authors then distinguish between outcomes rated critical and important:

For now, it would suffice to say that decisions regarding the overall quality of evidence supporting a recommendation may depend on which outcomes are designated as critical for making the decision (e.g., those rated 7, 8, or 9, on the 9-point scale mentioned earlier) and which are not. (p. 397)

Thus, the GRADE system asks guideline developers to classify outcomes into importance categories, without concern that patients might differ in how they would weigh the outcomes.

5

Reasonable Care with Sample Data

This chapter continues discussion of reasonable patient care under uncertainty, now considering use of sample data to inform decision making. Because of its centrality to evidence-based medicine, I focus on the use of sample trial data in treatment choice. Moreover, having already addressed identification, I consider here only statistical imprecision, as has been the case in the statistical literature on trials. Readers interested in research that jointly considers statistical imprecision and identification problems should see Manski (2007b) and Stoye (2009, 2012).

Trial data aim to provide information about the outcome distributions that would occur if groups of patients with specified attributes were to be treated in a specified manner. Thus, they aim to be informative about group rather than personal states of nature. It is well appreciated that trials of finite size cannot definitively reveal outcome distributions. Statistical theory aims to characterize the information that trials provide.

Unfortunately, medical researchers have commonly applied concepts of statistical theory whose foundations are distant from treatment choice. As discussed in chapter 2, it has been common to use hypothesis tests to compare treatments. It has also been common to measure imprecision using confidence intervals, a concept that also is remote from decision making. By definition, a 95% confidence interval for an average treatment effect is a data-dependent interval that contains the true ATE with frequentist probability

0.95, across repeated samples. Statistical theory does not explain how a computed confidence interval should inform treatment choice.

The Wald (1950) development of statistical decision theory provides a coherent framework for use of sample data to make decisions. A body of recent research applies statistical decision theory to determine treatment choices that achieve adequate performance in all states of nature, in the sense of maximum regret. This chapter describes the basic ideas and findings, which provide an appealing practical alternative to use of hypothesis tests. I begin by describing the Wald theory.

5.1. Principles of Statistical Decision Theory

Wald considered the general problem of using sample data to make decisions. He posed the task as choice of a *statistical decision function*, which maps potentially available data into a choice among the feasible actions. Wald's seminal book is abstract, making it a difficult read. Ferguson (1967) and Berger (1985) provide rigorous but more accessible expositions.

Wald recommended ex ante evaluation of statistical decision functions as *procedures* applied as the sampling process is engaged repeatedly to draw independent data samples. The idea of a procedure transforms the original statistical problem of induction from a single sample into the deductive problem of assessing the probabilistic performance of a statistical decision function across realizations of the sampling process. Thus, the theory is frequentist.

Wald proposed that the decision maker evaluate a statistical decision function by the mean welfare it yields across realizations of the sampling process. His presentation differed semantically from the one that I use to describe treatment choice in that he defined loss to be the negative of welfare, took the objective to be minimization of loss rather than maximization of welfare, and used the term *risk* to denote mean loss across realizations of the sampling process. With these semantic distinctions, he prescribed a three-step decision process:

(1) Specify the set of feasible actions, the loss (negative welfare) function, and the state space. These basic concepts of decision theory are context specific. The set of feasible actions is commonly considered to be predetermined. The loss function and the state space are subjective. The former formalizes what the decision maker wants to achieve, and the latter expresses what states of nature he believes could possibly occur.

(2) Eliminate inadmissible statistical decision functions. A decision function is inadmissible if there exists another that yields at least as good mean sampling performance in every state of nature and strictly better mean performance in some state.

(3) Use some criterion to choose an admissible statistical decision function. Wald focused on the *minimax* criterion and on minimization of a subjective mean of the risk function (called *Bayes risk*). Savage (1951) proposed *minimax regret*.

Among decision criteria, maximization of subjective expected utility has been studied extensively. Statistical decision theorists usually call these Bayes decisions. This focuses attention on the Bayesian process of transforming a *prior* subjective distribution, determined before observing the sample data, into a *posterior* distribution after observing the data.

The Bayesian prescription for statistical inference is sometimes asserted to be antithetical to frequentist statistical theory, but Wald provided a clear frequentist perspective on Bayes decisions. He showed that minimization of Bayes risk, a frequentist decision criterion, yields the same decisions as occur if one performs Bayesian inference, combining the prior distribution with the data to form a posterior subjective distribution, and then chooses an action to minimize the posterior mean of expected loss. Berger (1985) gives an accessible proof.

Bayesian decision making is compelling when one feels able to place a credible subjective prior distribution on the state space. There exists a considerable body of work ranging across multiple disciplines that develops methods to help persons conceptualize uncertainty and express themselves in subjective probabilistic terms. See, for example, Savage (1971); Koriat, Lichtenstein, and Fischhoff (1980); Morgan and Henrion (1990); Manski (2004b); and Garthwaite, Kadane, and O'Hagan (2005).

Nevertheless, Bayesians have long struggled to provide guidance on specification of priors, and the matter continues to be controversial. See, for example, the spectrum of views regarding Bayesian analysis of randomized trials expressed by the authors and discussants of Spiegelhalter, Freedman, and Parmar (1994). The controversy suggests that inability to express a credible prior is common in actual decision settings.

When one finds it difficult to assert a credible subjective distribution, a reasonable way to act is to use a decision criterion that achieves adequate performance in all states of nature. The maximin and minimax-regret criteria provide two ways to formalize this idea. Wald's version of the maximin criterion chooses a decision function that minimizes maximum risk across all states; hence, Wald called it minimax rather than maximin. One may similarly apply the minimax-regret criterion with sample data. To do so, one defines the regret of a specified statistical decision function in a given state of nature to be the difference between the minimum risk achievable in that state and the risk obtained with the specified decision function.

SOME HISTORY, POST-WALD

The Wald framework for decision making with sample data has breathtaking generality. In principle, it enables comparison of all statistical decision functions whose risk functions exist. It enables comparison of alternative sampling processes as well as decision rules. It uses no asymptotic approximations. It applies whatever information the decision maker may have.

Given the appeal of statistical decision theory, one might anticipate that it would play a central role in modern statistics. However, this has not occurred. After publication of Wald (1950), a surge of important extensions and applications followed in the 1950s. Much research focused on best point prediction under square loss with sample data, analysis of which began with Hodges and Lehmann (1950). In this important case, regret is mean square error and the minimax-regret criterion yields a predictor that minimizes maximum mean square error across the state space.

However, this period of rapid development ended by the 1960s, except for Bayesian statistical decision theory. Bayesian analysis has continued to develop, but as a self-contained field of study disconnected from the Wald frequentist framework. Recent research in Bayesian statistics has focused more on the computational problem of transformation of priors into posteriors than on use of posteriors in decision making.

Why did statistical decision theory lose momentum long ago? One reason may have been the technical difficulty of the subject. It is easy to describe Wald's ideas, but applying them can be analytically and computationally demanding. Determination of admissible decision functions and minimax or minimax-regret rules is often difficult. Another reason may have been diminishing interest in decision making as the motivation for analysis of sample data. Modern statisticians tend to view their objectives as estimation and hypothesis testing rather than decision making.

I cannot be sure what role these or other reasons played in the vanishing of statistical decision theory from statistics in the latter part of the twentieth century. However, the near absence of the subject in mainstream journals and textbooks of the period is indisputable. I think this is unfortunate.

The recent research described in the next section aims to reinvigorate statistical decision theory, focusing on its application to treatment choice. Complement 5A provides a formal presentation in the relatively simple setting of a trial with two treatments and a population of observationally identical patients.

5.2. Recent Work on Statistical Decision Theory for Treatment Choice

Bayesian statistical decision theory has long been available as a methodology to design trials and to choose treatments with trial data. DeGroot (1970) provides a treatise on the subject. Canner (1970); Spiegelhalter et al. (1994); Cheng, Su, and Berry (2003); and Spiegelhalter (2004) study various aspects. As mentioned above, Bayesians have struggled to provide guidance on specification of priors, and the matter continues to be controversial. Perhaps as a result, Bayesian analysis is well known but not often used in evidence-based medicine. A limited exception is that the FDA has provided guidance permitting the use of Bayesian statistics in the design and analysis of clinical trials evaluating new medical devices; see US Food and Drug Administration (2010).

I describe here recent research that avoids specification of priors and instead studies treatment choice that achieves adequate performance in all states of nature, using maximum regret to measure performance across states. Contributions to this emerging literature include Manski (2004a, 2005, 2007a, 2007b); Schlag (2006); Stoye (2009, 2012); Manski and Tetenov (2016, 2019); and Kitagawa and Tetenov (2018).

The recent research adopts a population health perspective. It supposes that the objective of treatment choice is to maximize a social welfare function that sums treatment outcomes across a population of patients who may have heterogeneous treatment response. For example, the objective may be to maximize the five-year survival rate in a population of cancer patients or mean life span in a population with a chronic disease. In this setting, a statistical decision function uses the data to choose an allocation of patients to treatments. Using terminology introduced in Manski (2004a), such a function has been called a *statistical treatment rule (STR)*. The mean sampling performance of an STR across repeated samples is its *expected welfare*. In Wald's terminology, risk is the negative of expected welfare.

In the absence of a prior distribution on the state space, practical and conceptual reasons motivate study of minimax-regret rather than maximin decision making. Next, I explain why.

PRACTICAL APPEAL

Researchers have generally studied treatment choice with trial data on outcomes that have bounded range. Leading examples are cases where the outcome may be treatment success or failure. From a practical perspective, it has been found that treatment choice using the minimax-regret criterion behaves more reasonably than does choice using the maximin criterion.

Numerical methods may be required to determine the STR that precisely minimizes maximum regret. To simplify analysis, researchers have often studied the maximum regret of the *empirical success* (ES) rule, which chooses the treatment with the highest observed average outcome in the trial. The ES rule provides a simple and plausible way to use the results of a trial. The performance of the ES rule from the perspective of maximum regret was initiated by Manski (2004a). Subsequently, Schlag (2006) and Stoye (2009) showed that this rule either exactly or approximately minimizes maximum regret in common settings with two treatments when sample size is moderate.

In contrast, the maximin rule ignores the trial data, whatever they may be. When Savage (1951) stated that the maximin criterion is "ultrapessimistic," he went on to write: "it can lead to the absurd conclusion in some cases that no amount of relevant experimentation should deter the actor from behaving as though he were in complete ignorance" (p. 63). Savage did not flesh out this statement, but it is easy to show that this occurs with trial data. Manski (2004a) provides a simple example that is discussed in complement 5A.

CONCEPTUAL APPEAL

The conceptual appeal of using maximum regret to measure performance is that maximum regret quantifies how lack of knowledge of the true state of nature diminishes the quality of decisions. While the term "maximum regret" has become standard in the literature, it is important to keep in mind that this term is a shorthand for the maximum suboptimality of a decision criterion across the feasible states of nature. An STR with small maximum regret is uniformly near-optimal across all states.

Maximum regret is well-defined in general settings with multiple treatments and when patients have heterogeneous observable attributes that may be used to differentiate treatment. However, the concept is especially transparent when there are two treatments and the members of the patient population are observationally identical, all having the same observable attributes.

Suppose there are two feasible treatments, say A and B. In a state of nature where A is better, the regret of an STR is the product of the probability across repeated samples that the rule commits a Type I error (choosing B) and the magnitude of the loss in expected welfare that occurs when choosing B. Similarly, in a state where B is better, regret is the probability of a Type II error (choosing A) times the magnitude of the loss in expected welfare when choosing A.

Recall the critique in chapter 2 of the conventional use of hypothesis testing to choose a treatment. I called attention to the asymmetric attention to Type I and Type II error probabilities and the inattention to magnitudes of losses when errors occur. Evaluating treatment rules by regret overcomes both problems. Regret considers Type I and II error probabilities symmetrically and it measures the magnitudes of the losses that errors produce.

A particularly simple case occurs when there are two states of nature and when Type I and Type II errors yield equal losses in expected welfare, say L. Then the maximum regret of an STR is L times the maximum of its probabilities of Type I and Type II errors.

Suppose that sample size has been chosen to give 0.05 probability of Type I error and 0.20 probability of Type II error, using a conventional test. Consider the STR that uses this test to choose a treatment. The maximum regret of this "test rule" is L times 0.20. One can obtain a test rule with smaller maximum regret by enlarging the critical region for the test. Enlarging the critical region increases the probability of Type I error and reduces that of Type II error. Maximum regret decreases until one enlarges the critical region to the degree that it equalizes the probabilities of Type I and Type II errors.

Example

To illustrate, consider again the example of section 2.4, in which a conventional hypothesis test is used as an STR to choose between a status quo treatment for cancer and an innovation. There are two feasible states of nature in the example, with the innovation yielding mean life span of 1/3 year in one state and 5 years in the other. In the first state, the regret of this conventional test rule equals 1/30 of a year; that is, a 0.05 chance of a Type I error times a 2/3 of a year reduction in mean life span with improper choice of the innovation. In the second state, the regret of the test rule equals 4/5 of a year; that is, a 0.20 chance of a Type II error times a 4-year reduction in mean life span with improper choice of the status quo. Thus, the maximum regret of the test rule is 4/5 of a year.

Rather than use the conventional test rule to choose between the status quo and the innovation, one could seek an STR that has smaller maximum regret. Given the available trial data, a simple option would be to reverse the conventional probabilities of Type I and Type II; thus, one might use a test with a 0.20 chance of a Type I error and a 0.05 chance of a Type II error. In the first state, the regret of this unconventional test rule STR equals 2/15 of a year; that is, a 0.20 chance of a Type I error times a 2/3 of a year reduction in mean life span with improper choice of the innovation. In the second state, the regret of the unconventional test rule equals 1/5 of a year; that is, a 0.05 chance of a Type II error times a 4-year reduction in mean life span with improper choice of the status quo. Thus, the maximum regret of the unconventional test rule is 1/5 of a year.

In this example, the unconventional test rule delivers much smaller maximum regret than does the conventional test rule. Other STRs may perform even better.

5.3. Designing Trials to Enable Near-Optimal Treatment Choice

The research described above concerns use of existing trial data to make treatment choices. A complementary question asks how trials should be designed to inform treatment choice effectively. A conventional practice has been to choose sample sizes that yield specified statistical power, but power is at most loosely connected to effective treatment choice. A better idea would be to choose sample size to enable near-optimal treatment choice. I explain here.

USING POWER CALCULATIONS TO CHOOSE SAMPLE SIZE

The use of statistical power calculations to set sample sizes derives from the presumption that trial data will be used to test a specified null hypothesis against an alternative. A common practice is to use the outcome of a hypothesis test to recommend whether a patient population should receive a status quo treatment or an innovation. The usual null hypothesis is that the innovation is no better than the status quo and the alternative is that the innovation is better. If the null hypothesis is not rejected, it is recommended that the status quo treatment continue to be used. If the null is rejected, it is recommended that the innovation replace the status quo as the treatment of choice.

As discussed in chapter 2, the standard practice has been to perform a test that fixes the probability of rejecting the null hypothesis when it is correct; that is, the probability of a Type I error. Then sample size determines the probability of rejecting the alternative hypothesis when it is correct, the probability of a Type II error. The power of a test is defined as one minus the probability of a Type II error. The convention has been to choose sample sizes that yield specified power at some value of the effect size deemed clinically important.

Trials with samples too small to achieve small probabilities of Type II errors are called "underpowered" and are regularly criticized as scientifically useless and medically unethical. According to Halpern, Karlawish, and Berlin (2002, p. 358), "Because such studies may not adequately test the underlying hypotheses, they have been considered 'scientifically useless' and therefore unethical in their exposure of participants to the risks and burdens of human research." Trials with samples larger than needed to achieve conventional error probabilities are called "overpowered" and are sometimes criticized as unethical. As Altman (1980, p. 1336) notes, "A study with an overlarge sample may be deemed unethical through the unnecessary involvement of extra subjects and the correspondingly increased costs."

SAMPLE SIZE ENABLING NEAR-OPTIMAL TREATMENT CHOICE

From the perspective of treatment choice, an ideal objective for the design of trials would be to collect data that enable subsequent implementation of an optimal treatment rule in the patient population of interest; that is, a rule for use of trial data that always selects the best treatment, with no chance of error. Optimality is too strong a property to be achievable with finite sample size. However, near-optimal rules—ones with small maximum regret—exist when trials are large enough.

Manski and Tetenov (2016) investigate trial design that enables near-optimal treatment choices. We show that, given any $\varepsilon > 0$, *ε-optimal* rules exist when trials have large enough sample size. An ε-optimal rule has expected welfare, across repeated samples, within ε of the welfare of the best treatment in every state of nature. Equivalently, it has maximum regret no larger than ε.

We consider trials that draw predetermined numbers of subjects at random within groups stratified by patient attributes and treatments. We report exact results for the special case of two treatments and binary outcomes. We give simple sufficient conditions on sample sizes that ensure existence of ε-optimal treatment rules when there are multiple treatments and outcomes are bounded.

CHOOSING THE NEAR-OPTIMALITY THRESHOLD

Use of a near-optimality criterion to set sample sizes requires specification of a value for ε. The need to choose an effect size of interest when designing trials already arises in conventional practice, where the trial planner must specify the alternative hypothesis to be compared with the null. Manski and Tetenov suggest that a possible way to specify ε is to base it on the *minimum clinically important difference* (MCID) in the average treatment effect comparing alternative treatments.

Medical research has long distinguished between the statistical and clinical significance of treatment effects (Sedgwick, 2014). While the idea of clinical significance (sometimes called clinical importance or relevance) has been interpreted in various ways, many writers call an average treatment effect clinically significant if its magnitude is greater than a specified value deemed minimally consequential in clinical practice. The International Conference on Harmonisation (1999) put it this way: "The treatment difference to be detected may be based on a judgment concerning the minimal effect which has clinical relevance in the management of patients" (p. 1923).

Research articles reporting trial findings sometimes pose specific values of MCIDs when comparing alternative treatments for specific diseases. For example, in their study comparing drug treatments for hypertension, Materson et al. (1993) defined the outcome of interest to be the fraction of subjects who achieve a specified threshold for blood pressure. They took the MCID to be the fraction 0.15, stating that this is: "the difference specified in the study design to be clinically important" (p. 916). They reported groups of drugs "whose effects do not differ from each other by more than 15 percent."

TABLE 5.1. Minimum Sample Sizes per Treatment Enabling ε-Optimal Treatment Choice: Binary Outcomes, Two Treatments, Balanced Designs

ε	ES Rule	One-Sided 5% z-Test	One-Sided 1% z-Test
0.01	145	3488	7963
0.03	17	382	879
0.05	6	138	310
0.10	2	33	79
0.15	1	16	35

FINDINGS WITH BINARY OUTCOMES, TWO TREATMENTS, AND BALANCED DESIGNS

Determination of sample sizes that enable near-optimal treatment is simple in settings with binary outcomes (coded 0 and 1 for simplicity), two treatments, and a balanced design that assigns the same number of subjects to each treatment group. Manski and Tetenov (2016, table 1), reproduced here as table 5.1, provides exact computations of the minimum sample size that enables ε-optimality when a clinician uses one of three different treatment rules, for various values of ε.

The first column shows the minimum sample size (per treatment arm) that yields ε-optimality when a clinician uses the empirical success (ES) rule to make a treatment decision. The ES rule chooses the treatment with the better average outcome in the trial. The rule assigns half the population to each treatment if there is a tie. It is known that the ES rule minimizes maximum regret rule in settings with binary outcomes, two treatments, and balanced designs (Stoye, 2009).

The second and third columns display the minimum sample sizes that yield ε-optimality of rules based on one-sided 5% and 1% hypothesis tests. There is no consensus on what hypothesis test should be used to compare two proportions. Results are reported based on the widely used one-sided two-sample z-test, which is based on an asymptotic normal approximation (Fleiss, 1981).

The findings are remarkable. A sample as small as 2 observations per treatment arm makes the ES rule ε-optimal when ε = 0.1 and a sample of size 145 suffices when ε = 0.01. The minimum sample sizes required for ε-optimality of the test rules are orders of magnitude larger. If the z-test of size 0.05 is used, a sample of size 33 is required when ε = 0.1 and 3488 when ε = 0.01. The sample sizes must be more than double these values if the z-test of size 0.01 is used. Manski and Tetenov (2016) discuss the factors that underlie these findings.

IMPLICATIONS FOR PRACTICE

Based on their exact calculations and analytical findings using large-deviations inequalities, Manski and Tetenov conclude that sample sizes determined by clinically relevant near-optimality criteria tend to be much smaller than ones set by conventional statistical power criteria. Reduction of sample size relative to prevailing norms can be beneficial in multiple ways. Reduction of total sample size can lower the cost of executing trials, the time necessary to recruit adequate numbers of subjects, and the complexity of managing trials across multiple centers. Reduction of sample size per treatment arm can make it feasible to perform trials that increase the number of treatment arms and, hence, yield information about a wider variety of treatment options.

5.4. Reconsidering Sample Size in the MSLT-II Trial

Manski and Tetenov (2019) quantify the reduction in sample size in a particular setting, reconsidering a trial that compared aggressive treatment of patients with surveillance. The Multicenter Selective Lymphadenectomy Trial II (MSLT-II), discussed in complement 1A, compared lymph node dissection and nodal observation for certain melanoma patients; see Faries et al. (2017). Using a statistical power calculation, the MSLT-II investigators assigned 971 patients to dissection and 968 to observation.

Manski and Tetenov (2019) consider sample size from the perspective of near-optimal treatment choice. We assume a simple patient welfare function. Welfare with nodal observation equals 1 if a patient survives for three years and equals 0 otherwise. Welfare with dissection depends on whether a patient experiences lymphedema.

When a patient does not experience lymphedema, welfare with dissection equals 1 if the patient survives for three years and equals 0 otherwise. When a patient experiences lymphedema, welfare is lowered by a specified fraction h, whose value expresses the harm associated with lymphedema. Thus, a patient who experiences lymphedema has welfare 1 − h if he survives and −h if he does not survive.

The sample-size calculations in Manski and Tetenov (2016) concerned settings where treatments do not have side effects. Hence, they cannot be applied to MSLT-II or other trials comparing nodal observation and lymph node dissection. Manski and Tetenov (2019) develop a refined version of the earlier analysis that recognizes the possibility of side effects.

We determine a sample size that enables near-optimal treatment when $h = 0.2$ and $\varepsilon = 0.0085$. Setting $h = 0.2$ supposes that suffering from lymphedema reduces a patient's welfare by one-fifth relative to lymphedema-free survival. This quantification of the welfare loss produced by lymphedema is suggested by Cheville et al. (2010), who elicited from a group of patients their perspectives on the matter.

Setting $\varepsilon = 0.0085$ follows naturally from the way that the MSLT-II investigators performed their power calculation. They judged a difference of 5 percentage points in melanoma-specific survival to be a clinically meaningful loss in patient welfare, and they judged 0.17 to be an acceptable probability of Type II error. As discussed in section 5.2, regret equals the magnitude of welfare loss times the probability that the loss will occur. Thus, the MSLT-II investigators judged $0.17 \times 0.05 = 0.0085$ to be an acceptable level of regret.

When $h = 0.2$ and $\varepsilon = 0.0085$, we find that near-optimal treatment is achievable if one sets $N = 488$ and assigns an equal number of patients to each treatment arm; that is, 244 to observation and 244 to dissection. This sample size is much smaller than the 1,939 subjects who were enrolled in MSLT-II.

6

A Population Health Perspective on Reasonable Care

I observed in chapter 1 that a prominent argument for adherence to CPGs has been to reduce "unnecessary" or "unwarranted" variation in clinical practice. The meaning of these adjectives is clear when guideline developers have rational expectations, so optimization of patient care is feasible. A feature of optimal care is that all patients with the same observed attributes receive the same treatment. Hence, variation in the care of observationally similar patients is suboptimal.

I observed in chapter 4 that the argument for uniform treatment of similar patients loses some of its power when clinicians choose patient care under uncertainty. There is no uniquely optimal choice among undominated actions. Different clinicians may reasonably interpret the available evidence in different ways and may reasonably use different decision criteria to choose treatments. There is no prima facie reason to view variation in choice among undominated treatments as unnecessary or unwarranted.

The argument for treatment variation strengthens when one considers patient care as a population health problem rather than from the perspective of a clinician treating an individual patient. Manski (2007a, 2009) shows that randomly varying the treatment of patients with the same observed attributes can provide valuable error protection and information under uncertainty. That is, it may be useful to diversify treatment choice. This chapter explains.

Before proceeding, I note that the term *population health* is sometimes used interchangeably with *public health*, but Kindig and Stoddart (2003) distinguish between the two. The former term seems more appropriate for the subject of this chapter.

6.1. Treatment Diversification

A long-standing economic perspective when considering population health is to hypothesize a planner who treats a population of patients. The planner's objective is to maximize utilitarian social welfare, adding up patient welfare outcomes across the population. For example, the planner may want to maximize the survival rate or the mean life span of patients who suffer from a life-threatening disease.

A planner who has rational expectations for patient outcomes would make the same decisions as would clinicians optimizing the treatment of individual patients. As discussed in chapter 1, patients would be divided into groups having the same observed attributes. All patients in an attribute group would be given the care that yields the highest within-group mean welfare. Thus, patients with the same observed attributes would be treated uniformly.

The population health perspective may differ from that of the clinician when patients are treated under uncertainty. Suppose that the feasible treatments are A and B. A clinician treating an individual patient can only choose one treatment or the other. A planner can diversify treatment, allocating some fraction of a patient population to A and the remainder to B. Treatment diversification is useful because it enables a planner to avoid gross errors that would occur if all patients were inadvertently given an inferior treatment.

Treatment diversification is analogous to financial diversification, a familiar recommendation for portfolio allocation under uncertainty. A financial portfolio is diversified if an investor allocates positive fractions of wealth to different investments. Diversification enables an investor facing uncertain asset returns to limit the potential negative consequences of placing "all eggs in one basket."

The finance literature on portfolio allocation shows that an investor seeking to maximize subjective expected utility chooses to diversify if the probability distribution of returns has sufficient spread and if the investor is sufficiently "risk averse," utility being a sufficiently concave function of the return to the investment. Treatment diversification by a health planner can be studied in the same manner.

Manski (2007a, 2009) takes a different approach, studying treatment allocation using the minimax-regret criterion. The central result is that when there are two undominated treatments, a planner using the minimax-regret criterion always chooses to diversify. The specific fraction of patients assigned to each treatment depends on the available knowledge of treatment response.

Complement 6A formalizes the planning problem and explains the specific treatment allocation that minimizes maximum regret. I provide a simple example here, drawn from Manski (2007a, ch. 11).

TREATING X-POX

The example describes a dire but hopefully hypothetical scenario. Suppose that a new disease called x-pox is sweeping a community. Imagine that it is impossible to avoid infection. If untreated, infected persons always die. Thus, the entire population will die in the absence of effective treatment.

Suppose that researchers propose two treatments, say A and B. The researchers know that one treatment is effective, but they do not know which one. They know that administering both treatments in combination is fatal. Thus, a person will survive if and only if she is administered the effective treatment alone. There is no time to experiment to learn which treatment is effective. Everyone must be treated right away.

Suppose that a public health agency must decide how to treat the community. The agency wants to maximize the survival rate of the population. It can select one treatment and administer it to everyone. Then the entire population will either live or die. Or it can give one treatment to some fraction of the community and the other treatment to the remaining fraction. Then the survival rate will be one of the two chosen fractions. If half the population receives each treatment, the survival rate is certain to be 50 percent.

What should the agency do? It could give everyone the same treatment and hope to make the right choice, recognizing the possibility that the outcome may be calamitous. Or it could give half the population each treatment, ensuring that half the community lives and half dies.

One can argue reasonably for either alternative. The principles of decision theory discussed in chapter 4 can be used to motivate either course of action. There are two states of nature in the x-pox example. Treatment

A is effective in one state and B is effective in the other. All treatment allocations are undominated. Allocating a higher fraction of patients to A improves welfare if A is the better treatment, and allocating a higher fraction to B improves welfare if B is better. Thus, there exists no allocation that yields higher welfare in both states of nature.

The planner might use any of the three decision criteria discussed in chapter 4—expected welfare, maximin, and minimax regret—to choose a treatment allocation. Complement 6B shows that a planner who places subjective probabilities on the two states of nature and evaluates a treatment allocation by its subjective expected welfare would assign everyone to the treatment with the higher subjective probability of being effective. In contrast, the maximin and the minimax-regret criteria both prescribe that the planner should assign half the population to each treatment. Ex post, a planner who maximizes the expected survival rate finds that either everyone lives, or everyone dies. One who maximizes the minimum survival rate or minimizes maximum regret achieves a survival rate of one-half with certitude.

Although the maximin and minimax-regret criteria deliver the same treatment allocation in this example, the two criteria are not the same in general. They more typically yield different choices. To see this, let us amend the description of the x-pox problem by adding a third state of nature in which neither treatment is effective. It can be shown that adding this third state does not affect the choices made by a planner who maximizes expected welfare or minimizes maximum regret. However, all treatment allocations now solve the maximin problem. The reason is that there now exists a state of nature in which everyone dies, regardless of treatment.

One might ask what happens if the planner wants to maximize some increasing transformation of the population survival rate rather than the survival rate per se. Researchers in finance often suppose that reducing the return on a portfolio by 1 percent subtracts more from an investor's welfare than raising the return by 1 percent adds to welfare. Similarly, in the x-pox example, one may feel that reducing the survival rate of the population by 1 percent subtracts more from social welfare than raising the survival rate by 1 percent adds to welfare.

Manski (2009) shows that changing the social welfare function in this manner affects the three decision criteria differentially. The maximin allocation is unaffected. The MR allocation may change, but it remains diversified. The expected welfare allocation may be unaffected or may become diversified, depending on the specifics of the welfare transformation and the subjective probabilities that the planner places on the states of nature.

6.2. Adaptive Diversification

The preceding discussion considered a one-time choice, in which a planner allocates treatments to one cohort of patients. Now consider a planner who makes treatment decisions in a sequence of periods, facing a new group of patients each period. The planner may observe the outcomes of early decisions and use this evidence to inform treatment later. Diversification is advantageous for learning treatment response because it generates randomized experiments. As evidence accumulates, the planner can revise the fraction of patients assigned to each treatment in accord with the available knowledge. I have called this *adaptive diversification*.

Adaptive diversification might be achieved by a sufficiently risk-averse Bayesian planner who updates his prior subjective distribution on treatment response after observing the outcomes of each cohort of patients. A planner who does not want to specify a subjective distribution on treatment response can use the *adaptive minimax-regret (AMR)* criterion. In each period, this criterion applies the static MR criterion using the information available at the time. It is adaptive because successive cohorts may receive different allocations as knowledge of treatment response increases over time.

The AMR criterion is normatively appealing because it treats each cohort as well as possible, in the MR sense, given the available knowledge. It does not ask the members of one cohort to sacrifice for the benefit of future cohorts. Nevertheless, the diversification of treatment performed for the benefit of the current cohort enables learning about treatment response.

The fractional allocations produced by the AMR criterion are randomized experiments, so it is natural to ask how application of AMR differs from conventional trials. There are important differences in the fraction and composition of the population randomized into treatment. The AMR criterion randomizes treatment of all observationally similar patients. In contrast, the treatment groups in trials typically are small fractions of the patient population. Moreover, as discussed in chapter 2, trials draw subjects from pools of persons who volunteer to participate and who meet specific conditions, such as the absence of comorbidities. Hence, trials reveal the distribution of treatment response within certain subpopulations of patients, not within the full population.

ADAPTIVE TREATMENT OF A LIFE-THREATENING DISEASE

To illustrate the AMR criterion, I consider a hypothetical treatment-choice problem where the outcome of interest unfolds over multiple periods. As empirical evidence accumulates, the AMR treatment allocation changes accordingly.

When treating a life-threatening disease, the outcome of interest may be the number of years that a patient survives within some time horizon. Let the horizon be five years and let the outcome of interest be the number of years that a patient lives during the five years following receipt of treatment. This outcome gradually becomes observable as time passes. At the time of treatment, years of survival can take any of the values [0, 1, 2, 3, 4, 5]. A year later, one can observe whether a patient is still alive and hence can determine whether years survived equals zero or at least one year. And so on until year five, when the outcome is fully observable.

Table 6.1 presents hypothetical data on annual death rates following receipt of a status quo treatment or an innovation, labeled A and B. The entries show that 20 (10) percent of the patients who receive the status quo (innovation) die in the first year after treatment. In each of the subsequent years, the death rates are 5 percent and 2 percent, respectively. Overall, the entries imply that the mean numbers of years lived after treatment are 3.5 years with the status quo treatment and 4.3 years for the innovation.

I suppose that death rates under the status quo treatment are known at the outset from historical experience. However, the planner has no initial knowledge of death rates with the innovation. That is, he does not initially know whether the innovation will be disastrous, with all patients dying in the first year following treatment, or entirely successful, with all patients living five years or more. Then the initial bound on mean number of years lived with the innovation is [0, 5]. Applying the analysis in complement 6A, the AMR criterion initially allocates 0.70 of patients to the status quo and 0.30 to the innovation.

In year 1 the planner observes that, of the patients in cohort 0 assigned to the innovation, 10 percent died in the first year following treatment. This enables him to deduce that the fraction who live at least one year is 0.90. The planner uses this information to tighten the bound on mean years lived to [0.90, 4.50]. In each subsequent year the planner observes another annual

TABLE 6.1. Adaptive Diversification Treating a Life-Threatening Disease

Cohort or year (n or k)	Death rate in year k		Bound on mean years lived with innovation, cohort n	AMR allocation, cohort n	Maximum regret of AMR allocation, cohort n	Mean years lived, cohort n
	Status Quo	Innovation				
0			[0, 5]	0.30	1.05	3.74
1	0.20	0.10	[0.90, 4.50]	0.28	0.72	3.72
2	0.05	0.02	[1.78, 4.42]	0.35	0.60	3.78
3	0.05	0.02	[2.64, 4.36]	0.50	0.43	3.90
4	0.05	0.02	[3.48, 4.32]	0.98	0.02	4.28
5	0.05	0.02	[4.30, 4.30]	1	0	4.30

death rate, tightens the bound on mean years lived with the innovation, and recomputes the treatment allocation accordingly. The result is that the fractions of patients allocated to the innovation in years (1, 2, 3, 4) are (0.28, 0.35, 0.50, 0.98). In year 5 he becomes certain that the innovation is better than the status quo, and so allocates all patients to the innovation.

The final two columns of table 6.1 give the maximum regret and mean years lived of each cohort, both computed using the AMR treatment allocation. Maximum regret decreases to zero as information accumulates. Mean years lived initially declines slightly but increases thereafter.

6.3. The Practicality of Adaptive Diversification

IMPLEMENTATION IN CENTRALIZED HEALTH-CARE SYSTEMS

Implementation of adaptive diversification may be possible in centralized health-care systems where there exists a planning entity who chooses treatments for a broad patient population. Examples are the Military Health System in the United States, the National Health Service in the United Kingdom, and some private health maintenance organizations.

An open question is whether the relevant planners and patient populations would accept the idea. A possible objection is that fractional treatment allocations violate a version of the ethical principle calling for "equal treatment of equals." Fractional allocations are consistent with this principle in the ex-ante sense that observationally identical people have the same probability of receiving a specific treatment. They violate it in the ex-post sense that observationally identical persons ultimately receive different treatments.

There is precedent for societies to implement policies that use fractional treatment allocations. American examples include random drug testing and airport screening, calls for jury service, and the Green Card and Vietnam draft lotteries. In addition, present-day randomized trials implement fractional allocations. The norm has been to randomize volunteers who give informed consent, but the FDA has occasionally approved studies in which patients are randomized without consent; see Stein (2007).

Fractional treatment allocations made with the AMR criterion are consistent with prevailing standards of medical ethics. Medical ethics permit randomized trials under conditions of *clinical equipoise*; that is, when partial knowledge of treatment response prevents a determination that one treatment is superior to another. These are exactly the circumstances in which the AMR criterion yields a fractional allocation.

SHOULD GUIDELINES ENCOURAGE TREATMENT VARIATION UNDER UNCERTAINTY?

Purposeful adaptive diversification may be difficult to achieve in decentralized health-care systems where clinicians make individual treatment decisions. Clinicians may not be willing to intentionally randomize treatment except in trials, even though uncertainty implies clinical equipoise and so makes randomization consistent with medical ethics.

Suppose that adaptive diversification is not feasible. We can nevertheless question whether the medical community should discourage treatment variation when treatment response is uncertain. Instead, CPGs could encourage clinicians to recognize that treatment choice may reasonably depend on how one interprets the available evidence and on the decision criterion that one uses. The result could then be natural treatment variation that yields some of the error-limitation and learning benefits of adaptive diversification.

7

Managing Uncertainty in Drug Approval

This chapter continues discussion of patient care from a population health perspective by considering drug approval policy. In the United States, the approval process of the Food and Drug Administration determines whether a drug can legally be sold within the country. A similar process occurs in the European Union, with approval performed by the European Medicines Agency.

To obtain approval for a new drug, a pharmaceutical firm must provide to the FDA information on treatment response through the performance of randomized trials that compare the new drug with an existing treatment or a placebo. The FDA makes a binary (yes/no) approval decision after reviewing the findings of these trials. Approval decisions are made with incomplete knowledge of the effectiveness and side effects of new drugs. I describe how the FDA deals with uncertainty and suggest how the approval process might be improved.

7.1. The FDA Approval Process

The FDA process for drug approval begins with preclinical laboratory and animal testing of new compounds. Those that seem promising then go through three phases of trials, in which the new drug is compared with an accepted treatment or placebo. Phase 1 trials, which typically take about a year and are performed with twenty to eighty healthy persons, aim to determine the basic pharmacological action of the drug and the safety of different doses. Phase 2 trials, which usually take about two years and are performed with several hundred patients who are ill with a specific disease, give preliminary evidence on the efficacy and short-term side effects of the drug. Phase 3 trials, which usually take about three years and are performed with several hundred to several thousand patients ill with the disease, give further evidence on efficacy and side effects. Following completion of Phase 3, the firm files a New Drug Application and the FDA either approves or disapproves the drug (see US Food and Drug Administration, 2017b).

Although the FDA was created more than a century ago in the Pure Food and Drug Act of 1906, the present drug approval process is a more recent invention. From 1906 to 1938, the agency was unable to disapprove the sale of purported medicines. It only was able to outlaw labeling and other advertising that made unsupported claims of treatment safety and effectiveness. The Food, Drug, and Cosmetics Act of 1938 gave the FDA power to prohibit the sale of unsafe drugs, but without a requirement to assess effectiveness. The 1962 Amendments to the Act established the modern drug approval process, which requires pharmaceutical firms to demonstrate that new drugs are safe and effective through a series of randomized trials. See Peltzman (1973) and Temin (1980) for further discussion.

7.2. Type I and II Errors in Drug Approval

FDA evaluation of new drugs occurs with partial knowledge of treatment response. As a result, approval decisions are susceptible to two types of errors. Type I errors occur when new drugs that are inferior to accepted treatments are approved because they appear superior when evaluated using the available information. Type II errors occur when new drugs that are superior to accepted treatments are disapproved because they appear inferior when evaluated using the available information. Viscusi, Harrington, and Vernon (2005, ch. 22) provide a textbook discussion.

Type II errors commonly are permanent. The FDA provides no public documentation of rejected New Drug Applications. After a drug is disapproved, use ceases and no further data on treatment response are produced.

Some Type I errors eventually are corrected after drug approval through the FDA's post-market surveillance program, which analyzes data on the outcomes experienced when the drug is used in clinical practice (see US Food and Drug Administration, 2017c). However, the post-market surveillance program only aims to detect adverse side effects of approved drugs, not to assess their effectiveness in treating the conditions for which they are intended. The data available for post-market surveillance are limited by the fact that the FDA cannot compel a firm to perform new trials after a drug has been approved. The main instrument of post-market surveillance is the Adverse Event Reporting System, which encourages patients and physicians to submit reports of adverse side effects related to drug administration.

7.3. Errors Due to Statistical Imprecision and Wishful Extrapolation

A well-recognized potential source of errors in drug approval is the statistical imprecision of empirical findings from trials with finite samples of subjects. The FDA limits the frequency of statistical errors by requiring that trial sizes suffice to perform hypothesis tests with specified power. As discussed in chapter 5, there is much reason to question the logic of using power calculations to choose trial sizes. Nevertheless, conventional power calculations ensure that trial sizes are large enough to make statistical error a relatively minor concern.

The dominant determinants of errors in drug approval are the extrapolation problems discussed in chapter 2. The approval process essentially assumes that treatment response in the relevant patient population will be similar to response in the study population. It assumes that response in clinical practice will be similar to response with double-blinded treatment assignment. It assumes that drug effectiveness measured by outcomes of interest will be similar to effectiveness measured by surrogate outcomes. These assumptions may be unsubstantiated, but they have become enshrined by long use.

Although the FDA has adopted formal procedures to limit the frequency of statistical errors, it has not adopted procedures to cope with extrapolation problems. Instead, the approval process informally extrapolates from available trial data to the distribution of treatment response in real clinical settings. This practice has been criticized, but it persists.

Mullins et al. (2010) provide a cogent critique of the limited usefulness of the RCTs performed for FDA drug approval in predicting drug effectiveness in practice. Considering cancer drugs, they observe that experimentation on volunteers with minimal comorbidities makes study populations differ markedly from actual patient populations. They also observe that drugs approved by the FDA for one type of cancer are often used in practice to treat other types. Such "off-label" use of drugs is legal, even though it occurs without direct evidence of effectiveness.

FDA reliance on surrogate outcomes to assess treatment response has also been criticized, as in the articles of Fleming and Demets (1996), Davis et al. (2017), and Prasad (2017) quoted in chapter 2. A seemingly obvious solution would be to require that pharmaceutical firms perform trials of sufficient length to measure health outcomes of real interest. However, this has been thought politically infeasible. Psaty et al. (1999) write:

> One systematic approach is a requirement that, prior to their approval, new drug therapies for cardiovascular risk factors should be evaluated in large, long-term clinical trials to assess their effects on major disease end points. The use of surrogate outcomes is avoided, and the major health outcomes are known prior to marketing. Such an approach would slow the time to drug approval and may meet with resistance from pharmaceutical manufacturers. (p. 789)

Indeed, pharmaceutical firms eager for returns on investments and patient groups wanting access to new drugs have often advocated shortening rather than lengthening the present time to approval. In 1992, pressure for quicker approval decisions led to passage of the Prescription Drug User Fee Act. This legislation shortened the time that the FDA takes to review New Drug Applications, the expedited review being funded by user fees assessed on the firms seeking approval. The Act did not, however, shorten the duration of the trials performed in support of New Drug Applications.

7.4. FDA Rejection of Formal Decision Analysis

In 2012, the US Congress responded to continuing controversy about the drug approval process by requiring the FDA to implement a "structured risk-benefit assessment framework." The Food and Drug Administration Safety and Innovation Act of 2012 (Public Law 112-144) amended Section 505(d) of the Federal Food Drug and Cosmetic Act by requiring the FDA to

> implement a structured risk-benefit assessment framework in the new drug approval process to facilitate the balanced consideration of benefits and risks, a consistent and systematic approach to the discussion and regulatory decision-making, and the communication of the benefits and risks of new drugs.

I think it reasonable to interpret this language as requiring the FDA to approach drug approval as a formal problem of decision under uncertainty, as discussed in chapters 4 through 6. The FDA, however, has rejected use of formal decision analysis in drug approval.

Following enactment of the 2012 legislation, the FDA published a plan intended to fulfill the congressional requirement (US Food and Drug Administration, 2013). The agency responded skeptically to unnamed critics of the prevailing approval process who have recommended that the FDA use formal decision analysis. The agency stated, ex cathedra:

> In the past, some FDA stakeholders have indicated that there is room for improvement in the clarity and transparency of FDA's benefit-risk assessment in human drug review. When FDA approves a new product, the agency publishes the various relevant documents, such as discipline reviews (e.g. clinical, non-clinical, clinical pharmacology, biostatistics, and chemistry) and decision memoranda, on its website. While FDA takes great care to clearly explain the reasoning behind a regulatory decision in these documents, the clinical analysis may not always be readily understood by a broad audience who may wish to understand FDA's thinking. In addition, some have argued that drug regulatory decisions should be based on more formalized and quantitative approaches to benefit-risk assessment, including the assignment of weights to benefit and risk considerations. Others, however, are skeptical of fully quantitative approaches, and consider such attempts to be a highly subjective exercise that would add little clarity to regulatory decision making. (p. 1)

The agency then described and defended its preferred approach to drug approval. In a passage that I think important enough to quote in full, the agency rejected quantitative/formal decision analysis and argued for continuation of the "structured qualitative" approach that it has used in the past. The agency stated:

> In the last few years, as other disciplines such as decision science and health economics have been applied to drug regulatory decision-making, there has been much discussion among regulators, industry, and other stakeholders regarding "qualitative" versus "quantitative" approaches to benefit-risk assessment. The term "quantitative benefit-risk assessment" can have various meanings depending on who is asked. Some hold the view that a quantitative benefit-risk assessment encompasses approaches that seek to quantify benefits and risks, as well as the weight that is placed

on each of the components such that the entire benefit-risk assessment is quantitative. This approach is typical of quantitative decision modeling. It usually requires assigning numerical weights to benefit and risk considerations in a process involving numerous judgments that are at best debatable and at worst arbitrary. The subjective judgments and assumptions that would inevitably be embodied in such quantitative decision modeling would be much less transparent, if not obscured, to those who wish to understand a regulator's thinking. Furthermore, application of quantitative decision modeling seems most appropriate for decisions that are largely binary. Many benefit-risk assessments are more nuanced and conditional based on parameters that could be used to effectively manage a safety concern in the post-market setting. There is significant concern that reliance on a relatively complex model would obscure rather than elucidate a regulator's thinking.

These concerns have led FDA to the conclusion that the best presentation of benefit-risk considerations involves focusing on the individual benefits and risks, their frequency, and weighing them appropriately. FDA believes that this can be accomplished by a qualitative descriptive approach for structuring the benefit-risk assessment that satisfies the principles outlined earlier in this section, while acknowledging that quantification of certain components of the benefit-risk assessment is an important part of the process to support decision-making. FDA considers it most important to be clear about what was considered in the decision, to be as quantitative as possible in characterizing that information, and to fully describe how that information was weighed in arriving at a conclusion. Quantitative assessments certainly underpin the qualitative judgments of FDA's regulatory decisions, but FDA has adopted a structured qualitative approach that is designed to support the identification and communication of the key considerations in FDA's benefit-risk assessment and how that information led to the regulatory decision. (p. 4)

The FDA rejection of formal decision analysis in drug approval is reminiscent of the Institute of Medicine (2011) rejection of formal decision analysis in guideline development, cited in chapter 4. I observed in chapter 4 that formal analysis of patient care under uncertainty can contribute much to guideline development and to clinical decision making. It similarly can improve drug approval. The next section presents some ideas, drawing on the discussion of adaptive diversification in chapter 6.

7.5. Adaptive Partial Drug Approval

Adaptive diversification of drug treatment after FDA approval of new drugs could reduce the impact of Type I errors in drug approval, diversifying treatment choice and producing new post-market information on treatment response. However, adaptive diversification after drug approval would not reduce Type II errors. Health-care providers can only choose among the drugs that are approved by the FDA.

Two policy changes could reduce the incidence and impact of Type II errors. First, the federal government could amend the Food, Drug, and Cosmetics Act to enable specified health-care providers to treat their patients with drugs that have not received FDA approval. In return for exemption from the FDA approval process, these providers could be required to apply appropriate adaptive treatment rules and to report findings on treatment response.

Second, the FDA could replace its present approval process with one of adaptive partial drug approval. The permitted use of a new drug now has a sharp discontinuity at the date of the FDA approval decision. Beforehand, a typically tiny fraction of the patient population receives the new drug in trials. Afterward, use of the drug is unconstrained if approval is granted and zero if approval is not granted. An adaptive approval process would eliminate this discontinuity and instead permit use of a new drug to vary smoothly as evidence accumulates.

Full FDA implementation of adaptive diversification would require radical change in the American health-care system, but the agency could embrace some important features with relatively modest revision to the present drug approval process. I sketch such a revision below, which I proposed in Manski (2009). Others have independently made similar proposals, albeit without an explicit decision-theoretic motivation. See Eichler et al. (2012).

ADAPTIVE LIMITED-TERM SALES LICENSES

The revised drug approval process would begin, as at present, with a pharmaceutical firm performing preclinical testing followed by Phase 1 and 2 trials. It seems prudent to retain these preliminary stages of the approval process in close to their current form. The changes would appear in the subsequent Phase 3 trials and in the FDA decision process.

The duration of Phase 3 trials would be lengthened sufficiently to measure health outcomes of real interest, not just surrogate outcomes. The present binary approval decision following Phase 3 would be replaced by an adaptive process that monitors the trial while in progress and that periodically grants limited-term sales licenses. An adaptive limited-term sales license would permit a firm to sell no more than a specified quantity of the new drug over a specified period. Subject to this bound, treatment allocation would be determined by the decentralized pricing decisions of the pharmaceutical firm, coverage decisions of insurers, and treatment decisions of physicians and patients.

To enforce the upper bound requires a means to monitor sales of a new drug. This is most straightforward if the FDA places only an overall upper bound on sales, rather than distinct bounds on sales to patient groups with different attributes. If only an overall upper bound is imposed, then it suffices to monitor gross sales in pharmacies. If group-specific bounds are imposed, it is necessary to monitor the distribution of sales.

The duration of the license would depend on the schedule for reporting new findings in the trial. For example, if the firm reports updated outcome data to the FDA annually, then the licensing decision could be updated annually as well. On each iteration of the decision, the maximum quantity of drug that the firm is permitted to sell would be set by the FDA with the assistance of an expert advisory board, similar to those now used in drug approval. To give the licensing decision transparency and coherence, the FDA could compute the AMR treatment allocation with a specified social welfare function, using the available evidence to determine the allocation.

When the lengthened Phase 3 trial has been completed and the outcomes of health interest have been observed, the FDA would make a longer-term approval decision. If the drug is deemed safe and effective, the firm would be permitted to sell it with no quantity restriction. Further use would be prohibited otherwise. As in the current environment, the FDA would retain the right to rescind approval should new evidence warrant.

Post-market surveillance would be necessary because lengthening Phase 3 trials to measure health outcomes of interest may not suffice to determine with certainty whether the innovation is superior to the status quo. As with present Phase 3 trials, the lengthened trials would only reveal treatment response for volunteer subjects who comply with treatment and do not drop out of the trial. Moreover, unless the FDA changes its norms on blinding treatment assignment, the trials would not reveal treatment response in real clinical settings where patients and physicians know the assigned treatments.

OPEN QUESTIONS

An adaptive approval process using limited-term sales licenses is one among various ways that the FDA might improve the present approval process. The agency could also empower a subset of health-care providers to prescribe the drug prior to final approval. It could restrict treatment to patients with specified characteristics. These and other mechanisms warrant consideration.

An open question when comparing the current approval process with alternatives is how pharmaceutical firms respond to the incentives that any approval process puts in place. We don't know much about how the drug approval process affects the decisions of firms to perform basic research, initiate Phase 1 through 3 trials, and submit New Drug Applications. Consideration of these uncertainties about the impact of drug regulation policy is important, but beyond the scope of this book.

Conclusion

To conclude, I return to the question with which I began chapter 1: Should clinicians adhere to guidelines or exercise judgment? I cited commentaries in the medical literature that recommend adherence to guidelines. However, as we proceeded to investigate patient care under uncertainty, I cautioned against universal adherence to guidelines.

I noted in chapter 1 that the guidelines issued by different health organizations sometimes disagree. Hence, clinicians may have to use judgment to determine which guideline to follow. I emphasized that clinicians observe patient attributes that are not considered in guidelines. Hence, clinicians can personalize care to a greater degree than is possible with guidelines.

Chapter 2 questioned the predictions of treatment response used in evidence-based guideline development. I cautioned that evidence-based research may not use the available evidence effectively to inform patient care. Focusing on the conduct and analysis of randomized trials, I called attention to questionable methodological practices that have afflicted research on treatment response.

Guidelines usually call for uniform treatment of observationally similar patients. I observed in chapter 4 that the argument for uniform treatment loses some power when clinicians choose patient care under uncertainty. There being no uniquely optimal choice, different clinicians may reasonably interpret available evidence in different ways and may reasonably use different criteria to choose treatments.

Chapter 6 showed that the rationale for treatment variation strengthens when one considers patient care as a population health problem rather than from the perspective of a clinician treating an individual patient. I explained that adaptive diversification of treatment can be valuable under uncertainty.

Separating the Information and Recommendation Aspects of Guidelines

Motivated by some of these considerations, Manski (2013a) proposed separating two tasks of guideline development that have commonly been performed in conjunction. One task is to characterize medical knowledge. The other is to make recommendations for patient care. I continue to think that these tasks should be separated.

Having guideline development groups characterize the state of medical knowledge has substantial potential to improve clinical practice. Medical research potentially relevant to patient care is vast, it continues to grow rapidly, and it requires considerable expertise to interpret. It is not feasible for individual clinicians to keep up with medical research on their own. Synthesis by expert panels seems essential.

The problem is that current approaches to synthesis of medical research are less informative to clinicians than they should be. As documented in chapter 2, a huge deficiency is over-attention to internal validity and corresponding neglect of external validity. As explained in chapter 3, this asymmetry has manifested itself in quantification of statistical imprecision without corresponding quantification of the severity of identification problems. Another shortcoming, discussed in chapter 4, is that guideline panels recognize uncertainty only qualitatively and shun use of formal decision theory when considering how to cope with uncertainty. Chapter 7 pointed out that the FDA drug approval process manifests the same deficiencies.

Improvement is possible. As discussed in chapters 3 through 7, I urge that synthesis of knowledge should draw on all available evidence, experimental and observational. It should maintain assumptions that are sufficiently credible to be taken seriously. It should combine the evidence and assumptions to draw credible conclusions that quantify uncertainty appropriately.

I question whether guidelines should often make recommendations for patient care under uncertainty. Making recommendations asks guideline developers to aggregate the benefits and harms of care into a scalar measure of welfare. It requires them to specify a decision criterion to cope with partial knowledge. These activities might be uncontroversial if there were consensus about how welfare should be measured and what decision criterion should be used. However, care recommendations may be contentious if perspectives vary across clinicians, patients, and other relevant parties. Then the recommendations made by guideline developers may not embody the considerations that motivate actual care decisions.

A separate consideration, discussed in chapter 6, is that having all clinicians adhere to the same guidelines may be suboptimal from a population health perspective. It does not recognize the value of diversification as a means of avoiding gross errors in treatment. It fails to exploit the opportunity for learning that diversification provides.

Educating Clinicians in Care under Uncertainty

An alternative to having guidelines make care recommendations would be to enhance the ability of clinicians to make reasonable patient care decisions under uncertainty. It would be useful to introduce medical students to core concepts of uncertainty quantification (both statistical imprecision and identification) and to decision analysis as part of their basic education. However, I do not expect that this will suffice. The basic training of clinicians already covers a considerable array of subjects. Substantial additions to curricula may be difficult to achieve.

I expect that an important part of the solution will be to bring specialists in uncertainty quantification and decision analysis into the clinical team. Modern clinical practice commonly has a group of professionals jointly contribute to patient care. Surgeons and internists may work together, and in conjunction with nurses and technical personnel. However, existing patient care teams do not ordinarily draw on professionals having specific expertise in the framing and analysis of complex decision problems. Adding such professionals to clinical teams may be more beneficial to patient care than asking physicians to adhere to guidelines issued by distant organizations.

To instruct basic medical students and develop specialists in patient care under uncertainty will require that medical schools create and implement appropriate curricula. I urge medical educators to make it so.

Overview of Research on Lymph Node Dissection

1A.1. Sentinel Lymph Node Biopsy

The controversy regarding the desirability of lymph node dissection for patients with early-stage melanoma persisted with little evolution for fully one hundred years, until the development of sentinel lymph node biopsy by Morton et al. (1992). Faries (2018) put it this way:

> Credit for starting this controversy is generally given to Herbert Snow, who proposed "anticipatory gland excision" in *The Lancet* in 1892. During the 20th century, his proposal was tested in a series of randomized clinical trials evaluating elective lymph node dissection. No individual trial showed a statistically significant survival benefit, but several demonstrated benefits for sizeable subgroups. This left room within the available data for varied interpretation and ongoing convictions on both sides. The development of sentinel lymph node biopsy by Morton et al. disrupted this debate by enabling lymphatic staging to be completed by a low-morbidity procedure and avoiding complete dissection for the vast majority of patients. (p. 1)

The research reported by Morton et al. did not settle the controversy about how melanoma spreads. Nevertheless, it made an important contribution to patient care by substantially narrowing the circumstances in which a clinician might reasonably recommend lymph node dissection for patients with early-stage melanoma.

Morton et al. (1992) focused on the then common use of dissection as a diagnostic test providing information on potential spread of disease in patients classified as having stage I melanoma. This early stage of the disease is defined as follows by the AIM at Melanoma Foundation (2018): "Stage I melanoma is defined as a melanoma that is up to 2 mm thick. A Stage I melanoma may or may not have ulceration. There is no evidence the cancer has spread to lymph nodes or distant sites (metastasis)."

The contribution of Morton et al. was to present persuasive empirical evidence that *sentinel lymph node (SLN) biopsy*, a diagnostic test that is much less invasive than lymph node dissection, is equally informative about the absence of spread of the disease to the regional lymph nodes. They found no microscopic evidence of malignancy in the sentinel nodes of about 80 percent of their stage I patients, suggesting that metastasis has not occurred. They concluded that there is no reason to perform a lymph node dissection for these 80 percent of patients, leaving the procedure potentially useful only for the remaining 20 percent.

An SLN biopsy has two steps. A clinician first injects a traceable dye at the site of the primary melanoma, determines the regional basin(s) of lymph nodes that drain the site, and identifies the sentinel lymph node(s), a sentinel node being a node that is closest to the melanoma site. The typical finding is that the site drains to a single regional node basin with a single sentinel node, but occasionally drainage to two regional basins is detected. Moreover, a regional basin occasionally has more than one sentinel node. In any case, the clinician biopsies any detected sentinel node to determine if it contains malignant cells. Side effects of the dye injection and biopsy are generally minimal. Performance of the procedure does, however, have significant financial cost.

The logic underlying SLN biopsy is that malignant cells traveling through the lymphatic system should affect the sentinel node(s) before any other regional lymph nodes. Hence, a finding of no malignancy in the SLN biopsy should suffice to show the absence of malignancy anywhere in the regional node basin. The open question was whether this logic is empirically accurate.

The researchers found SLN biopsy to be a resounding success. For each of a consecutive series of 223 stage I melanoma patients treated at the John Wayne Cancer Institute, they injected the traceable dye, performed lymph node dissection on the relevant regional node basins, and biopsied all of the nodes removed. This enabled them to determine whether malignant cells were present in each node. Researchers found that presence of malignancy in a sentinel node was essentially a necessary condition for finding malignancy in any non-sentinel node. Hence, finding no malignancy in the sentinel cell essentially rules out the possibility of malignancy elsewhere in the regional lymph basin. In their abstract, Morton et al. (1992) summarized their work and findings this way:

The initial route of metastases in most patients with melanoma is via the lymphatics to the regional nodes. However, routine lymphadenectomy for patients with clinical stage I melanoma remains controversial because most of these patients do not have nodal metastases, are unlikely to benefit from the operation, and may suffer troublesome postoperative edema of the limbs. A new procedure was developed using vital dyes that permits intraoperative identification of the sentinel lymph node, the lymph node nearest the site of the primary melanoma, on the direct drainage pathway. The most likely site of early metastases, the sentinel node can be removed for immediate intraoperative study to identify clinically occult melanoma cells. We successfully identified the sentinel node(s) in 194 of 237 lymphatic basins and detected metastases in 40 specimens (21%). . . . Metastases were present in 47 (18%) of 259 sentinel nodes, while non-sentinel nodes were the sole site of metastasis in only two of 3079 nodes from 194 lymphadenectomy specimens that had an identifiable sentinel node, a false-negative rate of less than 1%. Thus, this technique identifies, with a high degree of accuracy, patients with early stage melanoma who have nodal metastases and are likely to benefit from radical lymphadenectomy. (p. 392)

As an econometrician, I find it intriguing that the Morton et al. study appears to have had considerable influence on treatment of melanoma even though it was not a randomized trial and the researchers reported no measures of statistical precision for their findings. The subjects were simply 223 consecutive patients treated at one treatment center. The Morton et al. (1992) article does not explain why the researchers performed their study on this number of subjects nor why they were consecutive patients. The researchers did not use any statistical theory to interpret their findings; they just reported numerical findings as in the abstract quoted above. Their article mentions extrapolation beyond their findings only briefly, stating:

The general applicability of this technique to community practice outside a regional melanoma center, such as the John Wayne Cancer Institute, where 400 new patients with cutaneous melanoma are evaluated each year, is worthy of discussion. (p. 398)

I conjecture that the medical community has found the study persuasive for several reasons, despite its deviation from the norms of evidence-based medical research. First, the study focused on a well-understood and accurately measured outcome, namely the presence or absence of malignant cells in lymph nodes. Second, the logic underlying SLN biopsy is based on accepted medical understanding of the operation of the lymphatic system in humans. Third, the empirical findings of the study were remarkably strong, with malignancy in non-sentinel nodes almost always co-occurring with malignancy in the sentinel node.

Introduction of SLN biopsy altered the long-standing controversy about choice between nodal observation and dissection, but it did not end it. The original controversy was replaced in the 1990s by two new open questions about care of patients with early-stage melanoma. First, should these patients be subject to clinical observation of their lymph nodes or should they undergo SLN biopsy? Second, when patients undergo SLN biopsy and malignancy is found in a sentinel node, should they then undergo immediate dissection of the remaining nodes in the relevant regional basin?

Research seeking to inform these choices has accumulated through performance of randomized trials and observational studies. Especially notable are the first and second Multicenter Selective Lymphadenectomy Trials (MSLT-I and MSLT-II). MSLT-I compared nodal observation with SLN biopsy, while MSLT-II compared observation and dissection for patients found to have malignancy in a sentinel node. These trials and other studies have provided important new information, yet controversy about reasonable patient care persists. I explain below.

1A.2. Observation or SLN Biopsy

MSLT-I commenced in 1994, completed enrollment of patients in 2001, reported findings after five years of follow-up in an interim report (Morton et al., 2006), and reported findings after ten years in its final report (Morton et al., 2014). The trial sought to enroll early-stage patients whose primary melanoma was of intermediate thickness or greater. The rationale for limiting the trial to patients meeting this criterion was that patients with thin primary melanomas rarely experience metastasis. Hence, they would rarely benefit from biopsy, but they would have to endure the procedure and cover the cost.

A total of 1,661 patients were randomly assigned to two experimental groups. The protocol called for the primary melanoma to be surgically removed in both groups. In the "observation group," removal of the melanoma was followed by postoperative nodal observation for ten years. In the "biopsy group," removal of the melanoma was accompanied by sentinel node biopsy.

The groups also differed regarding performance of lymph node dissection. Patients in the observation group would undergo dissection only if postoperative nodal observation yields clinical evidence of metastasis to a lymph node. Patients in the biopsy group would undergo dissection immediately if the SLN biopsy yields microscopic evidence of malignancy.

The researchers reported findings regarding three patient survival outcomes: melanoma-specific, disease-free, and distant disease-free survival. National Cancer Institute (2018) defines a disease-specific survival rate, such as melanoma-specific survival, as follows:

> The percentage of people in a study or treatment group who have not died from a specific disease in a defined period of time. The time period usually begins at the time of diagnosis or at the start of treatment and ends at the time of death. Patients who died from causes other than the disease being studied are not counted in this measurement.

It defines disease-free survival as "The length of time after primary treatment for a cancer ends that the patient survives without any signs or symptoms of that cancer." Distant disease-free survival is the length of time after treatment that the patient survives without spread of the disease to a body location distant from the primary melanoma, for a suitable definition of "distant."

The researchers analyzed the trial outcomes using conventional statistical methodology, with considerable attention to measures of statistical significance associated with hypothesis testing. Morton et al. summarized their ten-year conclusions as follows in the abstract of their 2014 article:

> Biopsy-based staging of intermediate-thickness or thick primary melanomas provides important prognostic information and identifies patients with nodal metastases who may benefit from immediate complete lymphadenectomy. Biopsy-based management prolongs disease-free survival for all patients and prolongs distant disease-free survival and melanoma-specific survival for patients with nodal metastases from intermediate-thickness melanomas. (p. 509)

They ended the article with this positive recommendation for patient care:

> These long-term results clearly validate the use of sentinel-node biopsy in patients with intermediate-thickness or thick primary melanomas. The procedure provides accurate and important staging information, enhances regional disease control, and, among patients with nodal metastases, appears to improve melanoma-specific survival substantially. (p. 608)

The MSLT-I findings have influenced clinical guidelines for melanoma treatment issued in the United States. The 2017 guideline released by the

American Society of Clinical Oncology (ASCO) and the Society of Surgical Oncology (SSO) recommends SLN biopsy for all patients whose primary melanoma has intermediate thickness and states that it may be recommended for patients with thick primary melanomas (Wong et al., 2017). To support these recommendations, the guideline panel cites the MSLT-I findings prominently. The panel also mentions more briefly a set of recent observational studies.

Enthusiasm for SLN biopsy in the United Kingdom appears considerably less strong than in the United States. Commentaries written by Torjesen (2013) and McGregor (2013) raise multiple criticisms of the procedure and of reliance on the MSLT-I findings. McGregor (2013) writes that SLN biopsy

> is also in routine use for melanoma in many countries, but without proven survival advantage to date. More importantly, it does not direct further management in melanoma because we have no effective adjuvant intervention as yet. (pp. 233–234)

British guidelines for treatment of melanoma differ from American ones. The American ASCO-SSO guideline recommends SLN biopsy unreservedly when the primary melanoma has intermediate thickness. In contrast, the guideline issued by the British National Institute of Health and Care Excellence (NICE) (2015) is hesitant, stating:

> Consider sentinel lymph node biopsy as a staging rather than a therapeutic procedure for people with stage IB-IIC melanoma with a Breslow thickness of more than 1 mm, and give them detailed verbal and written information about the possible advantages and disadvantages.

NICE goes on to list possible advantages and disadvantages, which explain why it considers biopsy to be a staging rather than therapeutic procedure. The first advantage relates to staging: "The operation helps to find out whether the cancer has spread to the lymph nodes. It is better than ultrasound scans at finding very small cancers in the lymph nodes." The first disadvantage relates to therapy: "The purpose of the operation is not to cure the cancer. There is no good evidence that people who have the operation live longer than people who do not have it."

The NICE statement that there is no good evidence of survival benefit contradicts the conclusion of Morton et al. (2014) that "Biopsy-based management prolongs disease-free survival for all patients and prolongs distant disease-free survival and melanoma-specific survival for patients with nodal metastases from intermediate-thickness melanomas." The difference in perspective between NICE and Morton et al. calls to mind the comment of Faries (2018) cited in section 1.1 of chapter 1: "it is interesting to note how often the same information has been used to support contradictory conclusions."

1A.3. Observation or Dissection after Positive SLN Biopsy

The MSLT-I protocol called for patients in the biopsy group to undergo dissection immediately if the SLN biopsy yields microscopic evidence of malignancy. MSLT-II compared dissection of the remaining regional nodes with the alternative of nodal observation. The subjects in the trial were patients with early-stage melanoma who had recently undergone SLN biopsy and who had obtained a positive finding of malignancy.

The trial commenced in 2004, completed enrollment of patients in 2014, and reported findings in Faries et al. (2017). The discussion section of the article explains the rationale for the trial this way:

> The management of regional lymph nodes has long been controversial in the treatment of many solid tumors, particularly melanoma. The MSLT-I confirmed the staging value of sentinel node biopsy and showed a therapeutic advantage of early treatment of nodal metastases among patients with intermediate-thickness melanoma. The findings of that trial provided support for the use of sentinel-node biopsy, which is now recommended in the guidelines of most national and professional organizations for the treatment of melanoma.
>
> However, in patients with sentinel-node metastases, the value of completion lymph-node dissection remains controversial. Since most such patients have all nodal metastases removed by means of the sentinel-node biopsy procedure, they cannot derive additional therapeutic value from completion lymph-node dissection. Even microscopic nonsentinel-node metastases portend a markedly worse prognosis, similar to that of patients with bulky, clinically diagnosed metastases than the prognosis in patients with metastases that are limited to the sentinel lymph nodes. Patients with nonsentinel-node metastasis may be unlikely to benefit from early dissection. Finally, completion lymph-node dissection is associated with higher morbidity than sentinel node biopsy alone, so an appraisal of the value of the procedure is important. (pp. 2217–2219)

A total of 1,939 patients were randomly assigned to the two experimental groups, 971 assigned to dissection and 968 to observation. Subjects enrolled near the beginning of the trial could be followed for up to ten years, but those enrolled near the end were followed for only three years before publication of the Faries et al. (2017) article. The median follow-up period was forty-three months. The Faries et al. article focuses primarily on survival in the three-year period following patient entry in the trial. It also reports findings on survival over longer time spans, but the number of subjects observed over longer spans decreases rapidly. The researchers reported findings regarding melanoma-specific and disease-free survival.

Faries et al. (2017) provide a nuanced discussion of their findings. They give a succinct conclusion in the abstract of their article, stating:

> Immediate completion lymph-node dissection increased the rate of regional disease control and provided prognostic information but did not increase melanoma-specific survival among patients with melanoma and sentinel-node metastases. (p. 2211)

The discussion section of the article elaborates and ends as follows:

> Overall, some value may be derived from immediate completion lymph-node dissection with regard to staging and an increased rate of regional disease control. However, this value comes at the cost of increased complications. (p. 2221)

A year before publication of Faries et al. (2017), findings were reported from a contemporaneous but much smaller German trial that was ended early following difficulties in recruiting subjects and other issues (Leiter et al., 2016). The researchers reported findings on distant metastasis-free survival three years after patient entry for 233 patients randomly assigned to observation and 240 to dissection. They found no survival benefit for dissection and noted a higher frequency of side effects. Given this conjunction of lack of patient benefit and higher patient cost, they interpreted the trial findings as a basis for recommending against dissection, writing:

> Although we did not achieve the required number of events, leading to the trial being underpowered, our results showed no difference in survival in patients treated with complete lymph node dissection compared with observation only. Consequently, complete lymph node dissection should not be recommended in patients with melanoma with lymph node micrometastases of at least a diameter of 1 mm or smaller. (p. 757)

Following publication of Faries et al. (2017) and Leiter et al. (2016), the updated ASCO-SSO guideline for treatment of melanoma (Wong et al.,

2017) made a nuanced recommendation that cites these two trials. Using the acronym CLND to denote completion lymph node dissection, the guideline states:

> CLND or careful observation are options for patients with low-risk micrometastatic disease, with due consideration of clinicopathological factors. For higher risk patients, careful observation may be considered only after a thorough discussion with patients about the potential risks and benefits of foregoing CLND. (p. 12)

Thus, the ASCO-SSO guideline takes a neutral position on dissection versus observation for low-risk patients. It suggests that dissection should be the norm for higher-risk patients, but observation may be considered.

When discussing MSLT-II and the German trial, the ASCO-SSO guideline panel was careful to caution regarding extrapolation of their findings beyond the study populations. The panel wrote that both trials

> were conducted in patient populations in which the observation group received frequent follow-up evaluations, including the use of serial nodal ultrasound. Consequently, results from these trials may have limited applicability in settings where patients are unable to undergo frequent follow-up evaluations or in patients who receive treatment at institutions that are not able to perform high-quality nodal ultrasonography. (Wong et al., 2017, p. 12)

The most recent British NICE guideline was released before publication of the findings of MSLT-II and the German trial. It is similarly nuanced, stating: "Consider completion lymphadenectomy for people whose sentinel lymph node biopsy shows micro-metastases and give them detailed verbal and written information about the possible advantages and disadvantages" (National Institute for Health and Care Excellence, 2015). The guideline goes on to list multiple advantages and disadvantages.

Formalization of Optimal Choice between Surveillance and Aggressive Treatment

Here is a simple formalization of the problem of optimal choice between surveillance and aggressive treatment. Let treatment $t = A$ denote surveillance and $t = B$ denote aggressive treatment. Let $y(A)$ and $y(B)$ be potential binary outcomes, with $y = 1$ denoting that the patient will develop the disease and $y = 0$ otherwise. Let (x, w) be the patient attributes observed by a clinician, x being the subset used to make evidence-based predictions. Let $P_{xw}(t) \equiv P[y(t) = 1 | x, w]$ be the probability that a patient with observed attributes (x, w) will develop the disease if the patient receives treatment t. A clinician has rational expectations if he knows $P_{xw}(A)$ and $P_{xw}(B)$.

The utility of each care option depends on whether a patient will or will not develop the disease. Let $u_{xw}(y, t)$ denote the expected utility of treatment t to a patient with attributes (x, w) in the presence of disease outcome y. The clinician chooses a care option without knowing the disease outcome.

The expected utility of each treatment t without knowledge of the disease outcome is

$$P_{xw}(t) \cdot u_{xw}(1, t) + [1 - P_{xw}(t)] \cdot u_{xw}(0, t). \qquad (1B.1)$$

Maximization of expected utility yields the optimal treatment rule

Choose A if
$$P_{xw}(A) \cdot u_{xw}(1, A) + [1 - P_{xw}(A)] \cdot u_{xw}(0, A)$$
$$\geq P_{xw}(B) \cdot u_{xw}(1, B) + [1 - P_{xw}(B)] \cdot u_{xw}(0, B),$$
Choose B if
$$P_{xw}(B) \cdot u_{xw}(1, B) + [1 - P_{xw}(B)] \cdot u_{xw}(0, B)$$
$$\geq P_{x}(A) \cdot u_{xw}(1, A) + [1 - P_{xw}(A)] \cdot u_{xw}(0, A). \qquad (1B.2)$$

A clinician who knows patient preferences and has rational expectations can implement the optimal treatment rule. In general, this rule cannot be implemented by a CPG that predicts disease development and assesses patient expected utility conditional only on attributes x rather than (x, w).

Decision rule (1B. 2) is simple, but it is instructive to discuss further simplifications that occur when treatment operates on disease in different ways. In some clinical settings, aggressive treatment may prevent disease development whereas surveillance does not; thus, $P_{xw}(B) = 0$ and $P_{xw}(A) > 0$. In other settings, treatment does not affect disease development but may affect the severity of illness when it occurs; thus, $P_{xw}(B) = P_{xw}(A)$, but $u_{xw}(1, A)$ may differ from $u_{xw}(1, B)$. I show below that, in settings of both types, calculation of a threshold probability of disease suffices to determine the optimal treatment.

1B.1. Aggressive Treatment Prevents Disease

Suppose that $P_{xw}(B) = 0$. Then (1B.2) reduces to

> Choose A if
> $$P_{xw}(A) \cdot u_{xw}(1, A) + [1 - P_{xw}(A)] \cdot u_{xw}(0, A) \geq u_{xw}(0, B),$$
> Choose B if
> $$u_{xw}(0, B) \geq P_{xw}(A) \cdot u_{xw}(1, A) + [1 - P_{xw}(A)] \cdot u_{xw}(0, A).$$
> (1B.3)

Hence, the optimal treatment depends on the magnitude of $P_{xw}(A)$ relative to the threshold value that equalizes the expected utility of the two treatments:

$$P^*_{xw}(A) \equiv \frac{u_{xw}(0, A) - u_{xw}(0, B)}{u_{xw}(0, A) - u_{xw}(1, A)}. \tag{1B.4}$$

It is generally reasonable to expect that surveillance yields higher expected utility when a patient will remain healthy rather than develop the disease; that is, $u_{xw}(0, A) > u_{xw}(1, A)$. Then surveillance is optimal when $P_{xw}(A) \leq P^*_{xw}(A)$ and aggressive treatment is optimal when $P_{xw}(A) \geq P^*_{xw}(A)$.

Inspection of (1B.4) shows that $P^*_{xw}(A) \leq 0$ if $u_{xw}(0, A) - u_{xw}(0, B) \leq 0$; that is, if surveillance yields lower expected utility than aggressive treatment when a patient will not develop the disease. Then aggressive treatment is the better option whatever the patient's probability of disease development may be. Contrariwise, $P^*_{xw}(A) \geq 1$ if $u_{xw}(0, B) \leq u_{xw}(1, A)$; that is, if the expected utility of aggressive treatment in the absence of disease is less than that of surveillance in the presence of disease. Then surveillance is always better. When $0 < P^*_{xw}(A) < 1$, the better care option varies with the probability of disease development.

1B.2. Aggressive Treatment Reduces the Severity of Disease

Suppose that $P_{xw}(A) = P_{xw}(B) \equiv P_{xw}$. Then (1B.2) reduces to

Choose A if
$$P_{xw} \cdot u_{xw}(1, A) + (1 - P_{xw}) \cdot u_{xw}(0, A)$$
$$\geq P_{xw} \cdot u_{xw}(1, B) + (1 - P_{xw}) \cdot u_{xw}(0, B).$$
Choose B if $\qquad\qquad$ (1B.5)
$$P_{xw} \cdot u_{xw}(1, B) + (1 - P_{xw}) \cdot u_{xw}(0, B)$$
$$\geq P_{xw} \cdot u_{xw}(1, A) + (1 - P_{xw}) \cdot u_{xw}(0, A).$$

Now the optimal treatment depends on the magnitude of P_{xw} relative to the threshold value that equalizes the expected utility of the two treatments:

$$P^*_{xw} = \frac{u_{xw}(0, A) - u_{xw}(0, B)}{[u_{xw}(0, A) - u_{xw}(0, B)] + [u_{xw}(1, B) - u_{xw}(1, A)]} . \qquad (1B.6)$$

It is often reasonable to suppose that surveillance yields higher expected utility when a patient will not develop the disease and that aggressive treatment yields higher utility when a patient will develop the disease; that is, $u_{xw}(0, A) > u_{xw}(0, B)$, and $u_{xw}(1, B) > u_{xw}(1, A)$. Then $0 < P^*_{xw} < 1$. Treatment A is optimal if $P_{wx} \leq P^*_{xw}$ and B is optimal if $P_{xw} \geq P^*_{xw}$.

Odds Ratios and Health Risks

In a well-known text on epidemiology, Fleiss (1981, p. 92) states that retrospective studies of disease do not yield policy-relevant predictions and so are "necessarily useless from the point of view of public health." Nevertheless, he goes on to say that "retrospective studies are eminently valid from the more general point of view of the advancement of knowledge." What Fleiss means in the first statement is that retrospective studies do not provide data that enable credible point estimation of *attributable risk*, a quantity of substantive interest in population health. The second statement means that retrospective studies enable credible point estimation of the *odds ratio*, a quantity that is not of substantive interest but that is widely reported in epidemiological research. I explain here, drawing on Manski (2007a, ch. 5).

The term "retrospective studies" refers to a sampling process that is also known to epidemiologists as *case-control* sampling and to econometricians studying behavior as *choice-based* sampling (Manski and Lerman, 1977). I call it *response-based* sampling here, as in Manski (2007a). Formally, consider a population each of whose members is described by covariates x and a response (or outcome) y. Consider inference on the response probabilities $P(y|x)$ when the population is divided into response strata and random samples are drawn from each stratum. This is response-based sampling.

In a simple case prevalent in epidemiology, y is a binary health outcome and x is a binary risk factor. Thus, $y = 1$ if a person becomes ill and $y = 0$ otherwise, while $x = 1$ if the person has the risk factor and $x = 0$ otherwise. In a classic example, y denotes the presence of lung cancer and x denotes whether a person is a smoker. Response-based sampling draws random samples of ill and healthy persons. This reveals the distributions of the risk factor among those who are ill and healthy; that is, $P(x|y = 1)$ and $P(x|y = 0)$. It does not reveal $P(y|x)$.

A basic concern of research in population health is to learn how the probability of illness varies across persons who do and who do not have a risk factor. Attributable risk is the difference in illness probability between these groups; that is, $P(y = 1|x = 1) - P(y = 1|x = 0)$. Another measure of the variation of illness with the risk factor is the ratio $P(y=1|x=1)/P(y=1|x=0)$, called *relative risk*.

Texts on epidemiology discuss both relative and attributable risk, but empirical research has focused on relative risk. This focus is hard to justify from the perspective of population health. The health impact of a risk factor presumably depends on the number of illnesses affected; that is, on attributable risk times the size of the population. The relative risk statistic is uninformative about this quantity.

For example, consider two scenarios. In one, the probability of lung cancer conditional on smoking is 0.12 and conditional on non-smoking is 0.08. In the other, these probabilities are 0.00012 and 0.00008. The relative risk in both scenarios is 1.5. Attributable risk is 0.04 in the first scenario and 0.00004 in the second. The first scenario is clearly much more concerning to population health than the second. The relative risk statistic does not differentiate the scenarios, but attributable risk does.

Given that attributable risk is more relevant to population health, it seems odd that epidemiological research has emphasized relative risk rather than attributable risk. Indeed, the practice has long been criticized; see Berkson (1958), Fleiss (1981, sec. 6.3), and Hsieh, Manski, and McFadden (1985). The rationale, such as it is, rests on the widespread use in epidemiology of response-based sampling.

The data generated by response-based sampling do not point-identify attributable risk. Fleiss (1981, p. 92) remarked that "retrospective studies are incapable of providing estimates" of attributable risk. Manski (2007a) proves that these data do yield a bound.

Cornfield (1951) showed that the data from response-based sampling point-identify the odds ratio, defined as $[P(y=1|x=1)/P(y=0|x=1)]/[P(y=1|x=0)/P(y=0|x=0)]$. He also observed that when $P(y=1)$ is close to zero, a condition called the "rare-disease" assumption, the odds ratio approximately equals relative risk. The rare-disease assumption is credible when considering some diseases. In such cases, epidemiologists have used the odds ratio as a point estimate of relative risk.

Cornfield's finding motivates the widespread epidemiological practice of using response-based samples to estimate the odds ratio and then invoking the rare-disease assumption to interpret the odds ratio as relative risk. Fleiss's statement that retrospective studies are "valid from the more general point of view of the advancement of knowledge" endorses this practice. Thus, use of the odds ratio to point-estimate relative risk sacrifices relevance for certitude.

The Ecological Inference Problem in Personalized Risk Assessment

Let each member of a population be characterized by an outcome y and by attributes (x, w). Suppose that data are available from two sampling processes, each of which has a severe missing data problem. One sampling process draws persons at random from the population and yields observable realizations of (y, x), but the corresponding realizations of w are not recorded. The other sampling process draws persons at random and yields observable realizations of (w, x), but the realizations of y are not recorded. These two sampling processes reveal the distributions P(y|x) and P(w|x). Political scientists and sociologists use the term *ecological inference* to describe the problem of inference on P(y|x, w) given knowledge of P(y|x) and P(w|x).

In the context of patient care, y is a health outcome of interest, x denotes patient attributes used in an evidence-based risk assessment tool, and w denotes further patient attributes observed by clinicians. The evidence-based tool reveals P(y|x). A clinician treating a patient with attributes (x = k, w = j) wants to know the "long" probability distribution P(y|x = k, w = j) that predicts outcomes conditional on this value of (x, w). The evidence-based predictor only reveals the "short" distribution P(y|x = k) that conditions just on x.

The Law of Total Probability relates the short and long distributions, making the identification problem transparent:

$$P(y|x=k) = P(w=j|x=k) \cdot P(y|x=k, w=j) + P(w \neq j|x=k) \cdot P(y|x=k, w \neq j).$$

Knowledge of P(y|x = k) alone reveals nothing about P(y|x = k, w = j), because any distribution P(y|x = k, w = j) satisfies the equation if P(w = j|x = k) = 0. Partial conclusions may be drawn if one has evidence revealing P(y|x = k) and P(w = j|x = k), provided that the latter is positive.

The joint identification region for $P(y|x=k, w=j)$ and $P(y|x=k, w \neq j)$ given knowledge of $P(y|x)$ and $P(w|x)$ is the set of pairs of long distributions that satisfy the Law of Total Probability. The practical challenge is to characterize the feasible distributions. Analysis is simple when outcome y is binary and one makes no assumptions that restrict $P(y|x, w)$. Then the identification region for $P(y=1|x=k, w=j)$ is the interval

$$P(y=1|x=k, w=j) \in [0, 1]$$
$$\cap \left[\frac{P(y=1|x=k) - P(w \neq j|x=k)}{P(w=j|x=k)}, \frac{P(y=1|x=k)}{P(w=j|x=k)} \right].$$

This result was sketched by Duncan and Davis (1953). A proof is given in Horowitz and Manski (1995).

When y is real-valued, there is no similarly simple characterization of the identification region for $P(y|x, w)$. However, Horowitz and Manski (1995) derive tractable expressions for the identification regions of the mean and quantiles of $P(y|x, w)$. Their findings for the mean are used in Manski (2018a) to compute the bounds on remaining life span reported there.

Tighter conclusions may be drawn if one combines knowledge of $P(y|x)$ and $P(w|x)$ with various assumptions. Manski (2018a) summarizes the literature and presents new findings.

Bounds on Success Probabilities with No Knowledge of Counterfactual Outcomes

Let A and B be two treatments. Let potential patient outcomes under these treatments be denoted y(A) and y(B), respectively. Suppose that these outcomes can take the value 0 (failure) or 1 (success). Suppose that some members of a study population receive treatment A and the remainder receive B. A researcher observes the treatment that each patient receives and the outcome the patient experiences. Thus, the researcher observes y(A) for patients who receive A and y(B) for those who receive B. Outcome y(B) is counterfactual for patients who receive A, and y(A) is counterfactual for those who receive B.

Let the objective be to learn the probabilities $P[y(A)=1]$ and $P[y(B)=1]$ of successful outcomes if all patients in the study population were to receive treatment A or B, respectively. Let z denote the treatment that a member of the study population receives. The observational study reveals the fractions of the study population who receive each treatment; that is, $P(z=A)$ and $P(z=B)$. It also reveals the fractions of successful outcomes for the patients who receive each treatment; that is, $P[y(A)=1|z=A]$ and $P[y(B)=1|z=B]$. The study does not reveal the counterfactual success probabilities for patients who receive each treatment. That is, it does not reveal $P[y(B)=1|z=A]$ and $P[y(A)=1|z=B]$.

These probabilities are related to each other by the Law of Total Probability, which gives

$$P[y(A)=1] = P[y(A)=1|z=A] \cdot P(z=A) + P[y(A)=1|z=B] \cdot P(z=B),$$
$$P[y(B)=1] = P[y(B)=1|z=A] \cdot P(z=A) + P[y(B)=1|z=B] \cdot P(z=B).$$

The observational study reveals the probabilities on the right-hand side of each equation, except for the counterfactual success probabilities

$P[y(A)=1|z=B]$ and $P[y(B)=1|z=A]$. These can take any values between zero and one. Hence, we obtain these bounds on the success probability for each treatment:

$$P[y(A)=1|z=A]\cdot P(z=A) \leq P[y(A)=1]$$
$$\leq P[y(A)=1|z=A]\cdot P(z=A) + P(z=B),$$
$$P[y(B)=1|z=B]\cdot P(z=B) \leq P[y(B)=1]$$
$$\leq P[y(B)=1|z=B]\cdot P(z=B) + P(z=A).$$

These findings imply a bound on the average treatment effect. The lower bound is obtained by setting the success probability for B at its lower bound and that for A at its upper bound. The upper bound on the ATE is determined analogously. Thus, the bound on the ATE is

$$P[y(B)=1|z=B]\cdot P(z=B) - P[y(A)=1|z=A]\cdot P(z=A) - P(z=B)$$
$$\leq P[y(B)=1] - P[y(A)=1] \leq P[y(B)=1|z=B]\cdot P(z=B)$$
$$+ P(Z=A) - P[y(A)=1|z=A]\cdot P(z=A).$$

Formalization of Reasonable Choice between Surveillance and Aggressive Treatment

This complement continues the analysis of complement 1B. There we considered choice between surveillance and aggressive treatment when aggressive treatment either prevents disease or reduces the severity of disease. In the former case, it was shown that surveillance of a patient with attributes (x, w) is optimal when $P_{xw}(A) \leq P^*_{xw}(A)$ and aggressive treatment is optimal when $P_{xw}(A) \geq P^*_{xw}(A)$, where $P^*_{xw}(A)$ is the threshold disease probability defined in (1B.4). An analogous result was proved in the latter case, with P_{xw} replacing $P_{xw}(A)$ and P^*_{xw} defined in (1B.6) replacing $P^*_{xw}(A)$.

Our concern now is decision making when a clinician does not know the precise value of $P_{xw}(A)$ or P_{xw}, but he can bound the risk of disease. It suffices to consider one of the two cases, as analogous results hold for the other. I focus here on the case where aggressive treatment reduces the severity of disease. Thus, consider decision making when a clinician does not know P_{xw} but can use available evidence and credible assumptions to conclude that $P_{xw} \in [P_{xwL}, P_{xwH}]$, where P_{xwL} and P_{xwH} are known lower and upper bounds.

There exists a dominant treatment if P^*_{xw} is not inside the interval $[P_{xwL}, P_{xwH}]$. Then t = A is sure to be optimal if $P_{xwH} \leq P^*_{xw}$ and t = B is sure to be optimal if $P^*_{xw} \leq P_{xwL}$. There exists no dominant treatment if P^*_{xw} is within $[P_{xwL}, P_{xwH}]$. Then there exist feasible values of P_{xw} that make only A optimal and other values that make only B optimal.

The Bayesian prescription for decision making places a subjective distribution on P_{xw} and maximizes subjective expected utility. Let π_{xw} denote the subjective mean that a Bayesian clinician holds for P_{xw}. A Bayesian clinician acts as if $P_{xw} = \pi_{xw}$.

The maximin criterion evaluates each action by the worst expected utility that it may yield, and it chooses an action with the least-bad worst expected utility. The worst feasible expected utilities under options A and

B occur when P_{xw} equals its upper bound P_{xwH}. Hence, the clinician acts as if $P_{xw} = P_{xwH}$. The maximin choice is A if $P_{xwH} \leq P^*_{xw}$ and B if $P_{xwH} \geq P^*_{xw}$.

The minimax-regret criterion evaluates each action by the worst reduction in expected utility that it may yield relative to the highest expected utility achievable. Let P_{xwM} denote the midpoint of the interval $[P_{xwL}, P_{xwH}]$. Manski (2018a) shows that the minimax-regret choice is the same as a clinician maximizing expected utility would make if he were to know that $P_{xw} = P_{xwM}$.

Treatment Choice as a Statistical Decision Problem

I formalize treatment choice as a statistical decision problem in the relatively simple setting of a classical trial with two treatments and a population of observationally identical patients. The presentation draws substantially on Manski (2007a, ch. 12). The research literature that I cite in the main text of chapter 5 also studies more general and complex settings with multiple treatments, patients who have heterogeneous observable covariates, and imperfect trials that only partially identify treatment response.

Suppose that a health planner must assign treatment A or B to each member of patient population J. Each patient $j \in J$ has response function $y_j(\cdot): T \rightarrow Y$ mapping treatments $t \in T$ into individual outcomes $y_j(t) \in R$. Let P denote the distribution of treatment response in the population.

The members of the population may respond heterogeneously to treatment, but they are observationally identical to the planner. For any $\delta \in [0, 1]$, the planner can allocate a fraction δ of patients to treatment B and $1 - \delta$ to A. The planner wants to choose δ to maximize an additive social welfare function

$$U(\delta, P) = E[y(A)] \cdot (1 - \delta) + E[y(B)] \cdot \delta = \alpha(1 - \delta) + \beta\delta = \alpha + (\beta - \alpha)\delta,$$

where $\alpha \equiv E[y(A)]$ and $\beta \equiv E[y(B)]$ are the mean outcomes if everyone were to receive treatment A or B, respectively. The quantity $\beta - \alpha$ is the average treatment effect (ATE) in the population. It is optimal to set $\delta = 1$ if the ATE is positive and $\delta = 0$ if the ATE is negative. The problem of interest is treatment choice when incomplete knowledge of P makes it impossible to determine the sign of the ATE.

Suppose that sample data are available. Let Q be the sampling distribution and Ψ be the sample space. For example, the data may be treatment response observed in a randomized trial. A statistical treatment rule (STR) is a function $\delta(\cdot): \Psi \rightarrow [0, 1]$ that maps sample data into a treatment allocation. The welfare realized with δ and data ψ is the random variable

$$U(\delta, P, \psi) = \alpha + (\beta - \alpha) \cdot \delta(\psi).$$

The state space $[(P_s, Q_s), s \in S]$ is the set of (P, Q) pairs that the planner deems possible. Suppose S contains at least one state such that $\alpha_s > \beta_s$ and another such that $\alpha_s < \beta_s$. Expected welfare in state s, the mean sampling performance of rule δ in this state, is

$$W(\delta, P_s, Q_s) = \alpha_s + (\beta_s - \alpha_s) \cdot E_s[\delta(\psi)].$$

Here $E_s[\delta(\psi)] \equiv \int_\Psi \delta(\psi) dQ_s(\psi)$ is the expected allocation of patients to treatment B, across repeated samples.

Rule δ is admissible if there exists no rule δ' such that $W(\delta', P_s, Q_s) \geq W(\delta, P_s, Q_s)$ for all $s \in S$ and $W(\delta', P_s, Q_s) > W(\delta, P_s, Q_s)$ for some s. The Bayes, maximin, and MR rules are as follows:

Bayes Rule: $\max\limits_{\delta \in [0,1]} \quad \int_S W(\delta, P_s, Q_s) d\pi(s),$

where π is a subjective distribution on the state space.

Maximin Rule: $\max\limits_{\delta \in [0,1]} \quad \min\limits_{s \in S} W(\delta, P_s, Q_s).$

Minimax-Regret Rule: $\min\limits_{\delta \in [0,1]} \quad \max\limits_{s \in S} [\max(\alpha_s, \beta_s) - W(\delta, P_s, Q_s)].$

5A.1. Choice between a Status Quo Treatment and an Innovation When Outcomes Are Binary

To illustrate in perhaps the simplest non-trivial setting, let the outcomes y be binary, taking the value zero if treatment fails and one if it succeeds. Let A be a status quo treatment and B be an innovation. Suppose that the planner knows the success probability $\alpha \equiv P[y(A) = 1]$ of the status quo treatment but not the success probability $\beta \equiv P[y(B) = 1]$ of the innovation. The planner wants to choose treatments to maximize the success probability.

A randomized trial is performed to learn about outcomes under the innovation, with N subjects randomly drawn from the population and assigned to treatment B. The observed trial outcomes are that n subjects realize outcome $y = 1$ and $N - n$ realize $y = 0$. In this setting, N indexes the sampling process and the number n of experimental successes is a sufficient statistic for the data.

The feasible STRs are functions $\delta(\cdot)$: $[0, \ldots, N] \to [0, 1]$ that map the number of experimental successes into a treatment allocation. The expected welfare of rule δ is

$$W(\delta, P, N) = \alpha + (\beta - \alpha) \cdot E[\delta(n)].$$

n is distributed binomial $\mathbf{B}[\beta, N]$, so

$$E[\delta(n)] = \sum_{i=0}^{N} \delta(i) \cdot f(n = i; \beta, N)$$

where $f(n = i; \beta, N) \equiv N![i! \cdot (N-i)!]^{-1} \beta^i (1 - \beta)^{N-i}$ is the probability of i successes. The only unknown determinant of expected welfare is β, so the state space S indexes the feasible values of β. Specifically, $\beta_s \equiv P_s[y(b) = 1]$.

It is reasonable in this setting to conjecture that admissible treatment rules should be ones in which the fraction of the population allocated to treatment B increases with n. It turns out that the admissible treatment rules are a simple subclass of these rules. A theorem of Karlin and Rubin (1956) shows that the admissible rules are the *monotone treatment rules*. Monotone rules assign all persons to the status quo if the experimental success rate is below some threshold and all to the innovation if the success rate is above the threshold. Thus, δ is admissible if and only if

$$\delta(n) = 0 \text{ for } n < n_0,$$
$$\delta(n) = \lambda \text{ for } n = n_0,$$
$$\delta(n) = 1 \text{ for } n > n_0,$$

for some $0 \leq n_0 \leq N$ and $0 \leq \lambda \leq 1$.

The collection of monotone treatment rules is a mathematically "small" subset of the space of all feasible treatment rules. Nevertheless, it still contains a broad range of rules. These include:

Data-Invariant Rules: These are the rules $\delta(\cdot) = 0$ and $\delta(\cdot) = 1$, which assign all persons to treatment A or B, respectively, whatever n may be.

Empirical Success Rule: An optimal treatment rule allocates all persons to treatment A if $\beta < \alpha$ and all to B if $\beta > \alpha$. The empirical success rule emulates the optimal rule by replacing β with its sample analog, the empirical success rate n/N.

Bayes Rule: The form of the Bayes rule depends on the prior subjective distribution placed on β. Consider the class of Beta priors, which form the conjugate family for a Binomial likelihood. Let $(\beta_s, s \in S) = (0, 1)$ and let the prior be Beta with parameters (c, d). Then the posterior mean for β is $(c+n)/(c+d+N)$. The resulting Bayes rule is

$$\delta(n) = 0 \quad \text{for } (c+n)/(c+d+N) < \alpha,$$
$$\delta(n) = \lambda \quad \text{for } (c+n)/(c+d+N) = \alpha, \quad \text{where } 0 \le \lambda \le 1,$$
$$\delta(n) = 1 \quad \text{for } (c+n)/(c+d+N) > \alpha.$$

Maximin Rule: Minimum expected welfare for rule δ is

$$\min_{s \in S} W(\delta, P_s, N) = \alpha + \min_{s \in S} (\beta_s - \alpha) \cdot E_s[\delta(n)].$$

$E_s[\delta(n)] > 0$ for all $\beta_s > 0$ and for all monotone rules except $\delta(\cdot) = 0$. When S contains states with $\beta_s < \alpha$, the maximin rule is $\delta(\cdot) = 0$. Thus, the maximin rule ignores the trial data on treatment response, whatever they may turn out to be.

Minimax-Regret Rule: The regret of rule δ in state s is

$$\max(\alpha, \beta_s) - \{\alpha + (\beta_s - \alpha) \cdot E_s[\delta(n)]\}$$
$$= (\beta_s - \alpha)\{1 - E_s[\delta(n)]\} \cdot 1[\beta_s \ge \alpha] + (\alpha - \beta_s) E_s[\delta(n)] \cdot 1[\alpha \ge \beta_s].$$

Thus, regret is the mean welfare loss when a member of the population is assigned the inferior treatment, multiplied by the expected fraction of the population assigned this treatment. The minimax-regret rule does not have an analytical solution, but it can be determined numerically. When all values of β are feasible, the minimax-regret rule is well approximated by the empirical success rule.

Minimax-Regret Allocation
of Patients to Two Treatments

Consider a population of patients, all of whom have observed attributes x. Suppose that a health planner's task is to allocate these patients between the treatments, say A and B. It simplifies analysis to suppose that the patient population is infinitely large. This idealization implies that if the planner randomly assigns a positive fraction of the patients to a treatment, the sub-population who receive this treatment is infinite. This eliminates sampling variation as an issue when comparing alternative treatment allocations and analyzing treatment response.

A treatment allocation is a $\delta_x \in [0, 1]$ that randomly assigns a fraction δ_x of these patients to treatment B and the remaining $1 - \delta_x$ to treatment A. Let $\alpha_x \equiv E[u(A)|x]$ and $\beta_x \equiv E[u(B)|x]$ be expected utility if all patients receive treatment A or B, respectively. Social welfare with allocation δ_x is $\alpha_x(1 - \delta_x) + \beta_x \delta_x$. The optimal treatment allocation is $\delta_x = 1$ if $\beta_x \geq \alpha_x$ and $\delta_x = 0$ if $\beta_x \leq \alpha_x$.

The planner chooses a treatment allocation choice under uncertainty if (α_x, β_x) is not known. To formalize the problem, let S index the feasible states of nature. Let the planner know that (α_x, β_x) lies in the set $[(\alpha_{xs}, \beta_{xs}), s \in S]$. This state space is the set of values that the planner concludes are feasible when he combines available empirical evidence with assumptions he finds credible to maintain.

Partial knowledge is unproblematic for decision making if $(\alpha_{xs} \geq \beta_{xs}, s \in S)$ or if $(\alpha_{xs} \leq \beta_{xs}, s \in S)$; then $\delta_x = 0$ is optimal in the former case and $\delta_x = 1$ in the latter. However, all $\delta_x \in [0, 1]$ are undominated if $\alpha_{xs} > \beta_{xs}$ for some values of s and $\alpha_{xs} < \beta_{xs}$ for other values. I consider this situation. The analysis is applicable whenever $[(\alpha_{xs}, \beta_{xs}), s \in S]$ is bounded. Denote the extreme values as $\alpha_{xL} \equiv \min_{s \in S} \alpha_{xs}$, $\beta_{xL} \equiv \min_{s \in S} \beta_{xs}$, $\alpha_{xU} \equiv \max_{s \in S} \alpha_{xs}$, and $\beta_{xU} \equiv \max_{s \in S} \beta_{xs}$.

The regret of allocation δ_x in state of nature s is the difference between the maximum achievable welfare and the welfare achieved with this allocation. Maximum welfare in state s is $\max(\alpha_{xs}, \beta_{xs})$. Hence, δ_x has regret $\max(\alpha_{xs},$

$\beta_{xs}) - [\alpha_x(1 - \delta_x) + \beta_x \delta_x]$. The minimax-regret criterion computes the maximum regret of each allocation over all states and chooses one to minimize maximum regret. Thus, the criterion is

$$\min_{\delta_x \in [0, 1]} \quad \max_{s \in S} \quad \max(\alpha_{xs}, \beta_{xs}) - [\alpha_x(1 - \delta_x) + \beta_x \delta_x].$$

Manski (2007a, 2009) prove that the MR criterion always diversifies treatment when the optimal treatment is not known. Let $S_x(A)$ and $S_x(B)$ be the subsets of S on which treatments A and B are superior; that is, $S_x(A) \equiv \{s \in S: \alpha_{xs} > \beta_{xs}\}$ and $S_x(B) \equiv \{s \in S: \beta_{xs} > \alpha_{xs}\}$. Let $M_x(A) \equiv \max_{s \in Sx(A)} (\alpha_{xs} - \beta_{xs})$ and $M_x(B) \equiv \max_{s \in Sx(B)} (\beta_{xs} - \alpha_{xs})$ be maximum regret on $S_x(A)$ and $S_x(B)$, respectively. The general result is

$$\delta_{xMR} = \frac{M_x(B)}{M_x(A) + M_x(B)}.$$

This is a diversified allocation because $M_x(A) > 0$ and $M_x(B) > 0$.

$M_x(A)$ and $M_x(B)$ simplify when $(\alpha_{xL}, \beta_{xU})$ and $(\alpha_{xU}, \beta_{xL})$ are feasible values of (α_x, β_x), as when the state space is rectangular. Then $M_x(A) = \alpha_{xU} - \beta_{xL}$ and $M_x(B) = \beta_{xU} - \alpha_{xL}$. Hence,

$$\delta_{xMR} = \frac{\beta_{xU} - \alpha_{xL}}{(\alpha_{xU} - \beta_{xL}) + (\beta_{xU} - \alpha_{xL})}.$$

Derivations for Criteria to Treat X-Pox

Section 6.1 described policy choice when different decision criteria are used to treat x-pox. This complement gives the derivations when there are two states of nature, say s and t. Treatment A is effective in state s and treatment B in state t.

6B.1. Maximization of Subjective Expected Welfare

The planner places subjective probabilities on the two states of nature and evaluates a treatment allocation by its expected welfare. Suppose that he places probability p on state t and $1-p$ on state s. Then the expected welfare from assigning a fraction d of the population to B and $1-d$ to A is $pd + (1-p)(1-d)$. If p is larger than ½, assigning everyone to treatment B maximizes expected welfare. If p is smaller than ½, assigning everyone to A maximizes expected welfare. If p equals ½, all treatment allocations yield the same expected welfare.

6B.2. Maximin

The planner evaluates a treatment allocation by the minimum welfare that it may yield. The welfare from assigning a fraction d of the population to treatment B and $1-d$ to A is known to be either d or $1-d$. Hence, the minimum welfare from this allocation is the minimum of d and $1-d$. The allocation that maximizes minimum welfare is $d=½$. Thus, a planner using the maximin criterion assigns ½ of the population to each treatment.

6B.3. Minimax Regret

In each state of nature, one can achieve full survival of the population by allocating everyone to the treatment that is effective in this state. Thus, the regret of a candidate treatment allocation equals one minus the survival rate achieved by this allocation. Formally, the regret from assigning a fraction d of the population to treatment B and $1-d$ to A is d in state s and $1-d$ in state t. Hence, the maximum regret of this allocation is $\max(d, 1-d)$. The allocation that minimizes maximum regret is $d = \frac{1}{2}$. Thus, a planner using the MR criterion assigns $\frac{1}{2}$ of the population to each treatment.

The findings that the MR criterion allocates $\frac{1}{2}$ the population to each treatment is a special case of the general result given in complement 6A. In the x-pox setting, $(\alpha_{xL}, \beta_{xU})$ and $(\alpha_{xU}, \beta_{xL})$ are feasible values of (α_x, β_x), being $(0, 1)$ and $(1, 0)$. Hence, the MR allocation is

$$\delta_{xMR} = \frac{\beta_{xU} - \alpha_{xL}}{(\alpha_{xU} - \beta_{xL}) + (\beta_{xU} - \alpha_{xL})} = \frac{1-0}{(1-0)+(1-0)} = \frac{1}{2}.$$

REFERENCES

Academy of Medical Sciences (2015). *Stratified, Personalised or P4 Medicine: A New Direction for Placing the Patient at the Centre of Healthcare and Health Education.* www.acmedsci.ac.uk /viewFile/56e6d483e1d21.pdf, accessed July 4, 2016.

Agency for Healthcare Research and Quality (2017). https://www.guideline.gov/, accessed August 18, 2017.

AIM at Melanoma Foundation (2018). "Stage I Melanoma." https://www.aimatmelanoma.org /stages-of-melanoma/stage-i-melanoma/, accessed January 27, 2018.

Altman, D. (1980). "Statistics and Ethics in Medical Research: III How Large a Sample?" *BMJ*, 281, 1336–1338.

Altman, D., and J. Bland (1994). "Statistics Notes: Diagnostic Tests 2: Predictive Values." *BMJ*, 309, 102.

American College of Cardiology (2017). ASCVD Risk Estimator Plus. http://tools.acc.org /ASCVD-Risk-Estimator-Plus/#!/calculate/estimate/, accessed October 14, 2017.

American Society of Clinical Oncology (2018). Risk Evaluation Models. https://www.asco.org /practice-guidelines/cancer-care-initiatives/genetics-toolkit/assessing-your-patient%E2% 80%99s-hereditary-1, accessed October 1, 2018.

Amir, E., O. Freedman, B. Seruga, and D. Evans (2010). "Assessing Women at High Risk of Breast Cancer: A Review of Risk Assessment Models." *Journal of the National Cancer Institute*, 102, 680–691.

Arias, E. (2015). *United States Life Tables, 2011*, National Vital Statistics Reports, 64, no. 11, Centers for Disease Control and Prevention. www.cdc.gov/nchs/data/nvsr64/nvsr64_11.pdf, accessed May 2, 2017.

Balke, A., and J. Pearl (1997). "Bounds on Treatment Effects from Studies with Imperfect Compliance." *Journal of the American Statistical Association*, 92, 1171–1177.

Barsky, R. (1998). *Noam Chomsky: A Life of Dissent.* Cambridge, MA: MIT Press.

Basu, A., and D. Meltzer (2007). "Value of Information on Preference Heterogeneity and Individualized Care." *Medical Decision Making*, 27, 112–127.

Beckett, N., R. Peters, A. Fletcher, et al. (2008). "HYVET Study Group. Treatment of Hypertension in Patients 80 Years of Age or Older." *New England Journal of Medicine*, 358, 1887–1898.

Berger, J. (1985). *Statistical Decision Theory and Bayesian Analysis*, 2nd edition. New York: Springer.

Berkson, J. (1958). "Smoking and Lung Cancer: Some Observations on Two Recent Reports." *Journal of the American Statistical Association*, 53, 28–38.

Bhattacharya, J., A. Shaikh, and E. Vytlacil (2012). "Treatment Effect Bounds: An Application to Swan-Ganz Catheterization." *Journal of Econometrics*, 168, 223–243.

Blümle, A., J. Meerpohl, G. Rücker, G. Antes, M. Schumacher, and E. von Elm (2011). "Reporting of Eligibility Criteria of Randomised Trials: Cohort Study Comparing Trial Protocols with Subsequent Articles." *BMJ*, 342: d1828. doi:10.1136/bmj.d1828.

Boston Area Anticoagulation Trial for Atrial Fibrillation Investigators (1990). "The Effect of Low-Dose Warfarin on the Risk of Stroke in Patients with Nonrheumatic Atrial Fibrillation." *New England Journal of Medicine*, 323, 1505–1511.

Buchwald, H., Y. Avidor, E. Braunwald, M. Jensen, W. Pories, K. Fahrbach, and K. Schoelles (2004). "Bariatric Surgery: A Systematic Review and Meta-analysis." *Journal of the American Medical Association*, 292, 1724–1737.

Camerer, C., and E. Johnson (1997). "The Process-Performance Paradox in Expert Judgment: How Can Experts Know So Much and Predict So Badly." In *Research on Judgment and Decision Making*, edited by W. Goldstein and R. Hogarth. Cambridge: Cambridge University Press.

Campbell, D. (1984). "Can We Be Scientific in Applied Social Science?." *Evaluation Studies Review Annual*, 9, 26–48.

Campbell, D., and J. Stanley (1963). *Experimental and Quasi-Experimental Designs for Research*. Chicago: Rand McNally.

Canner, P. (1970). "Selecting One of Two Treatments When the Responses Are Dichotomous." *Journal of the American Statistical Association*, 65, 293–306.

Caulley, L., C. Balch, M. Ross, and C. Robert (2018). "Management of Sentinel-Node Metastasis in Melanoma." *New England Journal of Medicine*, 378, 85–88.

Chen, S., and G. Parmigiani (2007). "Meta-Analysis of *BRCA1* and *BRCA2* Penetrance." *Journal of Clinical Oncology*, 25, 1329–1333.

Cheng, Y., F. Su, and D. Berry (2003). "Choosing Sample Size for a Clinical Trial Using Decision Analysis." *Biometrika*, 90, 923–936.

Cheville, A., M. Almoza, J. Courmier, and J. Basford (2010). "A Prospective Cohort Study Defining Utilities Using Time Trade-Offs and the Euroqol-5D to Assess the Impact of Cancer-Related Lymphedema." *Cancer*, 116, 3722–3731.

Claus, E., N. Risch, and W. Thompson (1994). "Autosomal Dominant Inheritance of Early-Onset Breast Cancer. Implications for Risk Prediction." *Cancer*, 73, 643–651.

Clemen, R. (1989). "Combining Forecasts: A Review and Annotated Bibliography." *International Journal of Forecasting*, 5, 559–583.

Connors, A., T. Speroff, N. Dawson, C. Thomas, F. Harrell, D. Wagner, N. Desbiens, et al. (1996). "The Effectiveness of Right Heart Catheterization in the Initial Care of Critically Ill Patients." *Journal of the American Medical Association*, 276, 889–897.

Cook, R., and V. Farewell (1996). "Multiplicity Considerations in the Design and Analysis of Clinical Trials." *Journal of the Royal Statistical Society Series A*, 159, 93–110.

Cornfield, J. (1951). "A Method of Estimating Comparative Rates from Clinical Data. Applications to Cancer of the Lung, Breast, and Cervix." *Journal of the National Cancer Institute*, 11, 1269–1275.

Crits-Christoph, P., L. Siqueland, J. Blaine, A. Frank, L. Luborsky, L. Onken, L. Muenz, et al. (1999). "Psychosocial Treatments for Cocaine Dependence." *Archives of General Psychiatry*, 56, 493–502.

Davis, C., H. Nasi, E. Gurpinar, E. Poplavska, A. Pinto, and A. Aggarwal (2017). "Availability of Evidence of Benefits on Overall Survival and Quality of Life of Cancer Drugs Approved by European Medicines Agency: Retrospective Cohort Study of Drug Approvals 2009–13." *BMJ*, 359, doi:10.1136/bmj.j4530.

Dawes, R., R. Faust, and P. Meehl (1989). "Clinical Versus Actuarial Judgment." *Science*, 243, 1668–1674.

DeGroot, M. (1970). *Optimal Statistical Decisions*. New York: McGraw-Hill.

DerSimonian, R., and N. Laird (1986). "Meta-Analysis in Clinical Trials." *Controlled Clinical Trials*, 7, 177–188.

Domchek, S., A. Eisen, K. Calzone, J. Stopfer, A. Blackwood, and B. Weber (2003). "Application of Breast Cancer Risk Prediction Models in Clinical Practice." *Journal of Clinical Oncology*, 21, 593–601.

Duncan, O., and B. Davis (1953). "An Alternative to Ecological Correlation." *American Sociological Review*, 18, 665–666.

Dunnett, C. (1955). "A Multiple Comparison Procedure for Comparing Several Treatments with a Control." *Journal of the American Statistical Association*, 50, 1096–1121.

Eddy, D. (1984). "Physician Practice: The Role of Uncertainty." *Health Affairs*, 3, 74–89.

Eggermont A., and R. Dummer (2017). "The 2017 Complete Overhaul of Adjuvant Therapies for High-Risk Melanoma and Its Consequences for Staging and Management of Melanoma Patients." *European Journal of Cancer*, 86, 101–105.

Eichler, H., K. Oye, L. Baird, E. Abadie, J. Brown, C. Drum, J. Ferguson, et al. (2012). "Adaptive Licensing: Taking the Next Step in the Evolution of Drug Approval." *Clinical Pharmacology & Therapeutics*, 91, 426–437.

Ezekowitz, M., S. Bridgers, K. James, N. Carliner, C. Colling, C. Gornick, H. Krause-Steinrauf, et al. (1992). "Warfarin in the Prevention of Stroke Associated with Nonrheumatic Atrial Fibrillation." *New England Journal of Medicine*, 327, 1406–1412.

Faries, M. (2018). "Completing the Dissection in Melanoma: Increasing Decision Precision." *Annals of Surgical Oncology*, https://doi.org/10.1245/s10434-017-6330-4.

Faries, M., J. Thompson, A. Cochran, R. Andtbacka, N. Mozzillo, J. Zager, T. Jahkola, et al. (2017). "Completion Dissection or Observation for Sentinel-Node Metastasis in Melanoma." *New England Journal of Medicine*, 376, 2211–2222.

Ferguson, T. (1967). *Mathematical Statistics: A Decision Theoretic Approach*. San Diego: Academic Press.

Fisher, E., J. Wennberg, T. Stukel, and S. Sharp (1994). "Hospital Readmission Rates for Cohorts of Medicare Beneficiaries in Boston and New Haven." *New England Journal of Medicine*, 331, 989–995.

Fisher, L., and L. Moyé (1999). "Carvedilol and the Food and Drug Administration Approval Process: An Introduction." *Controlled Clinical Trials*, 20, 1–15.

Fleiss, J. (1981). *Statistical Methods for Rates and Proportions*, 2nd edition. New York: Wiley.

Fleming, T., and D. Demets (1996). "Surrogate End Points in Clinical Trials: Are We Being Misled?" *Annals of Internal Medicine*, 125, 605–613.

Fowler, R., and D. Cook (2003). "The Arc of the Pulmonary Artery Catheter." *Journal of the American Medical Association*, 290, 2732–2734.

Freis, E., B. Materson, and W. Flamenbaum (1983). "Comparison of Propranolol or Hydrochlorothiazide Alone for Treatment of Hypertension, III: Evaluation of the Renin-Angiotensin System." *American Journal of Medicine*, 74, 1029–1041.

Gail, M., L. Brinton, D. Byar, D. Corle, S. Green, C. Shairer, and J. Mulvihill (1989). "Projecting Individualized Probabilities of Developing Breast Cancer for White Females Who Are Being Examined Annually." *Journal of the National Cancer Institute*, 81, 1879–1886.

Gail, M., and P. Mai (2010). "Comparing Breast Cancer Risk Assessment Models." *Journal of the National Cancer Institute*, 102, 665–668.

Garthwaite, P., J. Kadane, and A. O'Hagan (2005). "Statistical Methods for Eliciting Probability Distributions." *Journal of the American Statistical Association*, 100, 680–701.

Gartlehner, G., R. Hansen, D. Nissman, K. Lohr, and T. Carey (2006). "Criteria for Distinguishing Effectiveness from Efficacy Trials in Systematic Reviews." Technical Review 12, AHRQ Publication No. 06-0046. Rockville, MD: Agency for Healthcare Research and Quality.

Gassenmaier, M., T. Eigentler, U. Keim, M. Goebeler, E. Fiedler, G. Schuler, U. Leiter, et al. (2017). "Serial or Parallel Metastasis of Cutaneous Melanoma? A Study of the German Central Malignant Melanoma Registry." *Journal of Investigative Dermatology*, 137, 2570–2577.

Ginsburg, G., and H. Willard (2009). "Genomic and Personalized Medicine: Foundations and Applications." *Translational Research*, 154, 277–287.

Go, A., E. Hylek, Y. Chang, K. Phillips, L. Henault, A. Capra, N. Jensvold, J. Selby, and D. Singer (2003). "Anticoagulation Therapy for Stroke Prevention in Atrial Fibrillation: How Well Do Randomized Trials Translate into Clinical Practice?." *Journal of the American Medical Association*, 290, 2685–2692.

Go, A., D. Mozaffarian, V. Roger, E. Benjamin, J. Berry, W. Borden, D. Bravata, et al.; on behalf of the American Heart Association Statistics Committee and Stroke Statistics Subcommittee (2013). "Heart Disease and Stroke Statistics—2013 Update: A Report from the American Heart Association." *Circulation*, 127, e6–e245.

Goldberg, L. (1968). "Simple Models or Simple Processes? Some Research on Clinical Judgments." *American Psychologist*, 23, 483–496.

Goldberger, A. (1972). "Structural Equation Methods in the Social Sciences." *Econometrica*, 40, 979–1001.

Good, I. (1967). "On the Principle of Total Evidence." *British Journal for the Philosophy of Science*, 17, 319–321.

Groves, W., D. Zald, B. Lebow, B. Snitz, and C. Nelson (2000). "Clinical Versus Mechanical Prediction: A Meta-Analysis." *Psychological Assessment*, 12, 19–30.

Guyatt, G., A. Oxman, R. Kunz, D. Atkins, J. Brozek, G. Vist, P. Alderson, et al. (2011). "Grade Guidelines: 2. Framing the Question and Deciding on Important Outcomes." *Journal of Clinical Epidemiology*, 64, 395–400.

Guyatt, G., A. Oxman, G. Vist, R. Kunz, Y. Falck-Ytter, P. Alonso-Coello, and H. Schünemann (2008). "Grade: An Emerging Consensus on Rating Quality of Evidence and Strength of Recommendations." *BMJ*, 336, 924–926.

Halpern, S., J. Karlawish, and J. Berlin (2002). "The Continued Unethical Conduct of Underpowered Clinical Trials." *Journal of the American Medical Association*, 288, 358–362.

Higgins J., and S. Green (editors) (2011). *Cochrane Handbook for Systematic Reviews of Interventions*, Version 5.1.0, The Cochrane Collaboration. http://handbook-5-1.cochrane.org/, accessed August 31, 2017.

Hodges, E., and E. Lehmann (1950). "Some Problems in Minimax Point Estimation." *Annals of Mathematical Statistics*, 21, 182–197.

Horowitz, J., and C. Manski (1995). "Identification and Robustness with Contaminated and Corrupted Data." *Econometrica*, 63, 281–302.

——— (1998). "Censoring of Outcomes and Regressors due to Survey Nonresponse: Identification and Estimation Using Weights and Imputations." *Journal of Econometrics*, 84, 37–58.

——— (2000). "Nonparametric Analysis of Randomized Experiments with Missing Attribute and Outcome Data." *Journal of the American Statistical Association*, 95, 77–84.

Hoyt, D. (1997). "Clinical Practice Guidelines." *American Journal of Surgery*, 173, 32–34.

Hsieh, D., C. Manski, and D. McFadden (1985). "Estimation of Response Probabilities from Augmented Retrospective Observations." *Journal of the American Statistical Association*, 80, 651–662.

Institute of Medicine (2011). *Clinical Practice Guidelines We Can Trust*. Washington, DC: National Academies Press.

——— (2013). *Variation in Health Care Spending: Target Decision Making, Not Geography*. Washington, DC: National Academies Press.

International Conference on Harmonisation (1999). ICH E9 Expert Working Group. Statistical Principles for Clinical Trials: ICH Harmonized Tripartite Guideline. *Statistics in Medicine*, 18, 1905–1942.

Ioannidis, J. (2005). "Why Most Published Research Findings Are False." *PLoS Medicine*, 2, e124.

James, P., S. Oparil, B. Carter, W. Cushman, C. Dennison-Himmelfarb, J. Handler, D. Lackland, et al. (2014). "Evidence-Based Guideline for the Management of High Blood Pressure in Adults

Report from the Panel Members Appointed to the Eighth Joint National Committee (JNC 8)." *Journal of the American Medical Association*, 311, 507–520.

Karlin, S., and H. Rubin (1956). "The Theory of Decision Procedures for Distributions with Monotone Likelihood Ratio." *Annals of Mathematical Statistics*, 27, 272–299.

Karmali, K., D. Goff, H. Ning, and D. Lloyd-Jones (2014). "A Systematic Examination of the 2013 ACC/AHA Pooled Cohort Risk Assessment Tool for Atherosclerotic Cardiovascular Disease." *Journal of the American College of Cardiology*, 64, 959–968.

Kasumova, G., A. Haynes, and G. Boland (2017). "Lymphatic versus Hematogenous Melanoma Metastases: Support for Biological Heterogeneity without Clear Clinical Application." *Journal of Investigative Dermatology*, 137, 2466–2468.

Kindig, D., and G. Stoddart (2003). "What Is Population Health?" *American Journal of Public Health*, 93, 380–383.

Kitagawa, T. (2009). "Identification Region of the Potential Outcome Distributions under Instrument Independence." Cemmap Working Paper, University College London.

Kitagawa, T., and A. Tetenov (2018). "Who Should Be Treated? Empirical Welfare Maximization Methods for Treatment Choice." *Econometrica*, 86, 591–616.

Koriat, A., S. Lichtenstein, and B. Fischhoff (1980). "Reasons for Confidence." *Journal of Experimental Psychology: Human Learning and Memory*, 6, 107–118.

Leiter, U., R. Stadler, C. Mauch, W. Hohenberger, N. Brockmeyer, C. Berking, C. Sunderkötter, et al. (2016). "Complete Lymph Node Dissection Versus No Dissection in Patients with Sentinel Lymph Node Biopsy Positive Melanoma (DeCOG-SLT): A Multicentre, Randomised, Phase 3 Trial." *Lancet Oncology*, 17, 757–767.

Mandelblatt, J., K. Cronin, S. Bailey, D. Berry, H. de Koning, G. Draisma, H. Huang, et al. (2009). "Effects of Mammography Screening Under Different Screening Schedules: Model Estimates of Potential Benefits and Harms." *Annals of Internal Medicine*, 151, 738–747.

Manski, C. (1989). "Anatomy of the Selection Problem." *Journal of Human Resources*, 24, 343–360.

——— (1990a). "The Use of Intentions Data to Predict Behavior: A Best Case Analysis." *Journal of the American Statistical Association*, 85, 934–940.

——— (1990b). "Nonparametric Bounds on Treatment Effects." *American Economic Review Papers and Proceedings*, 80, 319–323.

——— (1994). "The Selection Problem." In *Advances in Econometrics, Sixth World Congress*, edited by C. Sims, 143–170. Cambridge, UK: Cambridge University Press.

——— (1995). *Identification Problems in the Social Sciences*. Cambridge, MA: Harvard University Press.

——— (1997). "Monotone Treatment Response." *Econometrica*, 65, 1311–1334.

——— (2003). *Partial Identification of Probability Distributions*. New York: Springer.

——— (2004a). "Statistical Treatment Rules for Heterogeneous Populations." *Econometrica*, 72, 221–246.

——— (2004b). "Measuring Expectations." *Econometrica*, 72, 1329–1376.

——— (2005). *Social Choice with Partial Knowledge of Treatment Response*. Princeton, NJ: Princeton University Press.

——— (2007a). *Identification for Prediction and Decision*. Cambridge, MA: Harvard University Press.

——— (2007b). "Minimax-Regret Treatment Choice with Missing Outcome Data." *Journal of Econometrics*, 139, 105–115.

——— (2008). "Studying Treatment Response to Inform Treatment Choice." *Annales D'Économie et de Statistique*, 91/92, 93–105.

——— (2009). "Diversified Treatment under Ambiguity." *International Economic Review*, 50, 1013–1041.

———— (2010). "Vaccination with Partial Knowledge of External Effectiveness." *Proceedings of the National Academy of Sciences*, 107, 3953–3960.

———— (2011). "Interpreting and Combining Heterogeneous Survey Forecasts." In *Oxford Handbook on Economic Forecasting*, edited by M. Clements and D. Hendry, 457–472. Oxford: Oxford University Press.

———— (2013a). *Public Policy in an Uncertain World*. Cambridge, MA: Harvard University Press.

———— (2013b). "Diagnostic Testing and Treatment under Ambiguity: Using Decision Analysis to Inform Clinical Practice." *Proceedings of the National Academy of Sciences*, 110, 2064–2069.

———— (2016). "Interpreting Point Predictions: Some Logical Issues." *Foundations and Trends in Accounting*, 10, 238–261.

———— (2017). "Mandating Vaccination with Unknown Indirect Effects." *Journal of Public Economics Theory*, 19, 603–619.

———— (2018a). "Credible Ecological Inference for Medical Decisions with Personalized Risk Assessment." *Quantitative Economics*, 9, 541–569.

———— (2018b). "Reasonable Patient Care under Uncertainty." *Health Economics*, 27, 1397–1421.

———— (2019a). "The Lure of Incredible Certitude." *Economics and Philosophy*, forthcoming.

———— (2019b). "Meta-Analysis for Medical Decisions." National Bureau of Economic Research Working Paper W25504.

Manski, C., and S. Lerman (1977). "The Estimation of Choice Probabilities from Choice Based Samples." *Econometrica*, 45, 1977–1988.

Manski, C., and D. Nagin (1998). "Bounding Disagreements about Treatment Effects: A Case Study of Sentencing and Recidivism." *Sociological Methodology*, 28, 99–137.

Manski, C., and J. Pepper (2000). "Monotone Instrumental Variables: With an Application to the Returns to Schooling." *Econometrica*, 68, 997–1010.

Manski, C., and A. Tetenov (2016). "Sufficient Trial Size to Inform Clinical Practice." *Proceedings of the National Academy of Sciences*, 113, 10518–10523.

———— (2019). "Trial Size for Near-Optimal Treatment: Reconsidering MSLT-II." *The American Statistician*, 73, 305–311.

Materson, B., D. Reda, W. Cushman, B. Massie, E. Freis, M. Kochar, R. Hamburger, et al. (1993). "Single-Drug Therapy for Hypertension in Men: A Comparison of Six Antihypertensive Agents with Placebo." *New England Journal of Medicine*, 328, 914–921.

Mayo Clinic Staff (2018). "Warfarin Side Effects: Watch for Interactions." https://www.mayoclinic.org/diseases-conditions/deep-vein-thrombosis/in-depth/warfarin-side-effects/art-20047592, accessed May 25, 2018.

McGregor, J. (2013). "Too Much Surgery and Too Little Benefit? Sentinel Node Biopsy for Melanoma As It Currently Stands." *British Journal of Dermatology*, 169, 233–235.

McNees, S. (1992). "The Uses and Abuses of 'Consensus' Forecasts." *Journal of Forecasting*, 11, 703–710.

Meehl, P. (1954). *Clinical Versus Statistical Prediction: A Theoretical Analysis and a Review of the Evidence*. Minneapolis: University of Minnesota Press.

Meltzer, D. (2001). "Addressing Uncertainty in Medical Cost-Effectiveness: Implications of Expected Utility Maximization for Methods to Perform Sensitivity Analysis and the Use of Cost-Effectiveness Analysis to Set Priorities for Medical Research." *Journal of Health Economics*, 20, 109–129.

Mercuri, M., and A. Gafni (2011). "Medical Practice Variations: What the Literature Tells Us (Or Does Not) about What Are Warranted and Unwarranted Variations." *Journal of Evaluation in Clinical Practice*, 17, 671–677.

Morgan, G., and M. Henrion (1990). *Uncertainty: A Guide to Dealing with Uncertainty in Quantitative Risk and Policy Analysis*. New York: Cambridge University Press.

Morton, D., J. Thompson, A. Cochran, N. Mozzillo, R. Elashoff, R. Essner, O. Nieweg, et al. (2006). "Sentinel-Node Biopsy or Nodal Observation in Melanoma." *New England Journal of Medicine*, 355, 1307–1317.

Morton, D., J. Thompson, A. Cochran, N. Mozzillo, O. Nieweg, D. Roses, H. Hoekstra, et al. (2014). "Final Trial Report of Sentinel-Node Biopsy versus Nodal Observation in Melanoma." *New England Journal of Medicine*, 370, 599–609.

Morton, D., D. Wen, J. Wong, J. Economou, L. Cagle, F. Storm, L. Foshag, and A. Cochran (1992). "Technical Details of Intraoperative Lymphatic Mapping for Early Stage Melanoma." *Archives of Surgery*, 127, 392–399.

Mullahy, J. (2018). "Individual Results May Vary: Elementary Analytics of Inequality-Probability Bounds, with Applications to Health-Outcome Treatment Effects." *Journal of Health Economics*, 61, 151–162.

Mullins, D., R. Montgomery, and S. Tunis (2010). "Uncertainty in Assessing Value of Oncology Treatments." *Oncologist*, 15 (supplement 1), 58–64.

National Cancer Institute (2011). *Breast Cancer Risk Assessment Tool*. http://www.cancer.gov /bcrisktool/, accessed August 19, 2017.

——— (2018). *NCI Dictionary of Cancer Terms*. www.cancer.gov/publications/dictionaries /cancer-terms, accessed January 26, 2018.

National Comprehensive Cancer Network (2017). *Breast Cancer Screening and Diagnosis*, Version 1.2017. www.nccn.org/professionals/physician_gls/pdf/breast-screening.pdf, accessed March 8, 2018.

National Health Service (2015). *The NHS Atlas of Variation in Healthcare*. http://fingertips.phe .org.uk/profile/atlas-of-variation, accessed May 12, 2017.

National Institute for Health and Care Excellence (2015). "Melanoma: Assessment and Management," NICE Guideline [NG 14]. https://www.nice.org.uk/guidance/ng14/chapter /1-Recommendations#staging-investigations-2, accessed January 29, 2018.

Oeffinger, K., E. Fontham, R. Etzioni, A. Herzig, J. Michaelson, Y. Shih, L. Walter, et al. (2015). "Breast Cancer Screening for Women at Average Risk: 2015 Guideline Update from the American Cancer Society." *Journal of the American Medical Association*, 314, 1599–1614.

Pauly, M. (1980). "Physicians as Agents." In *Doctors and Their Workshops: Economic Models of Physician Behavior*, edited by M. Pauly, 1–16. Chicago: University of Chicago Press.

Peltzman, S. (1973). "An Evaluation of Consumer Protection Legislation: The 1962 Drug Amendments." *Journal of Political Economy*, 81, 1049–1091.

Phelps, C., and A. Mushlin (1988). "Focusing Technology Assessment Using Medical Decision Theory." *Medical Decision Making*, 8, 279–289.

Prasad, V. (2017). "Do Cancer Drugs Improve Survival or Quality of Life?" *BMJ*, 359. doi: https:// doi.org/10.1136/bmj.j4528.

President's Council of Advisors on Science and Technology (2008). "Priorities for Personalized Medicine." http://oncotherapy.us/pdf/PM.Priorities.pdf, accessed August 19, 2017.

Psaty, B., N. Weiss, C. Furberg, T. Koepsell, D. Siscovick, F. Rosendaal, N. Smith, et al. (1999). "Surrogate End Points, Health Outcomes, and the Drug-Approval Process for the Treatment of Risk Factors for Cardiovascular Disease." *Journal of the American Medical Association*, 282, 786–790.

Reiersol, O. (1945). "Confluence Analysis by Means of Instrumental Sets of Variables." *Arkiv fur Matematik, Astronomi Och Fysik*, 32A, no. 4, 1–119.

Rosenbaum, P. (1999). "Choice as an Alternative to Control in Observational Studies." *Statistical Science*, 14, 259–304.

Sackett, D. (1997). "Evidence-Based Medicine." *Seminars in Perinatology*, 21, 3–5.

Sarbin, T. (1943). "A Contribution to the Study of Actuarial and Individual Methods of Prediction." *American Journal of Sociology*, 48, 593–602.

——— (1944). "The Logic of Prediction in Psychology." *Psychological Review*, 51, 210–228.

Savage, L. (1951). "The Theory of Statistical Decision." *Journal of the American Statistical Association*, 46, 55–67.

——— (1971). "Elicitation of Personal Probabilities and Expectations." *Journal of the American Statistical Association*, 66, 783–801.

Schlag, K. (2006). "Eleven-Tests Needed for a Recommendation." European University Institute Working Paper ECO No. 2006/2.

Schünemann, H., S. Hill, M. Kakad, G. Vist, R. Bellamy, L. Stockman, T. Wisløff, et al. (2007). "Transparent Development of the WHO Rapid Advice Guidelines." *PloS Medicine*, 4, 786–793.

Sedgwick, P. (2014). "Clinical Significance Versus Statistical Significance." *BMJ*, 348: g2130. doi: 10.1136/bmj.g2130.

SHEP Cooperative Research Group (1991). "Prevention of Stroke by Antihypertensive Drug Treatment in Older Persons with Isolated Systolic Hypertension: Final Results of the Systolic Hypertension in the Elderly Program (SHEP)." *Journal of the American Medical Association*, 265, 3255–3264.

Singletary, K., and S. Gapstur (2001). "Alcohol and Breast Cancer: Review of Epidemiologic and Experimental Evidence and Potential Mechanisms." *Journal of the American Medical Association*, 286, 2143–2151.

Spiegelhalter, D. (2004). "Incorporating Bayesian Ideas into Health-Care Evaluation." *Statistical Science*, 19, 156–174.

Spiegelhalter D., L. Freedman, and M. Parmar (1994). "Bayesian Approaches to Randomized Trials" (with discussion). *Journal of the Royal Statistics Society Series A*, 157, 357–416.

Staessen, J. R. Fagard, L. Thijs, et al. (1997). "The Systolic Hypertension in Europe (Syst-Eur) Trial Investigators. Randomised Double-Blind Comparison of Placebo and Active Treatment for Older Patients with Isolated Systolic Hypertension." *Lancet*, 350, 757–764.

Stanley, T., and S. Jarrell (1989). "Meta-Regression Analysis: A Quantitative Method of Literature Surveys." *Journal of Economic Surveys*, 3, 161–170.

Stein, R. (2007). "Critical Care without Consent." *Washington Post*, May 27, A01.

Stoye, J. (2009). "Minimax Regret Treatment Choice with Finite Samples." *Journal of Econometrics*, 151, 70–81.

——— (2012). "Minimax Regret Treatment Choice with Attributes or with Limited Validity of Experiments." *Journal of Econometrics*, 166, 138–156.

Surowiecki, J. (2004). *The Wisdom of Crowds*. New York: Random House.

Susan G. Komen (2016). *Estimating Breast Cancer Risk*. ww5.komen.org/BreastCancer/GailAssessmentModel.html, accessed July 9, 2016.

Temin, P. (1980). *Taking Your Medicine: Drug Regulation in the United States*. Cambridge, MA: Harvard University Press.

Thompson, S., and J. Higgins (2002). "How Should Meta-Regression Analyses Be Undertaken and Interpreted?" *Statistics in Medicine*, 21, 1559–1573.

Torjesen, I. (2013). "Sentinel Node Biopsy for Melanoma: Unnecessary Treatment?" *BMJ*, 346:e8645. doi: 10.1136/bmj.e8645.

Tukey, J. (1962). "The Future of Data Analysis." *Annals of Mathematical Statistics*, 33, 1–67.

US Food and Drug Administration (2010). *Guidance for the Use of Bayesian Statistics in Medical Device Clinical Trials*. www.fda.gov/MedicalDevices/ucm071072.htm, accessed July 20, 2018.

——— (2013). *Structured Approach to Benefit-Risk Assessment in Drug Regulatory Decision-Making*. https://www.fda.gov/downloads/forindustry/userfees/prescriptiondruguserfee/ucm329758.pdf, accessed March 11, 2018.

——— (2014). *Statistical Guidance for Clinical Trials of Nondiagnostic Medical Devices*.

———— (2017a). "Multiple Endpoints in Clinical Trials." https://www.fda.gov/downloads/drugs/g uidancecomplianceregulatoryinformation/guidances/ucm536750.pdf, accessed September 13, 2018.

———— (2017b). "The FDA's Drug Review Process: Ensuring Drugs Are Safe and Effective." https://www.fda.gov/Drugs/ResourcesForYou/Consumers/ucm143534.htm, accessed March 11, 2018.

———— (2017c). "Postmarketing Surveillance Programs." https://www.fda.gov/Drugs/Guidance ComplianceRegulatoryInformation/Surveillance/ucm090385.htm, accessed March 11, 2018.

U.S. Preventive Services Task Force (2009). "Screening for Breast Cancer: U.S. Preventive Services Task Force Recommendation Statement." *Annals of Internal Medicine*, 151, 716–727.

Viscusi, K., J. Harrington, and J. Vernon (2005). *Economics of Regulation and Antitrust*, Cambridge, MA: MIT Press.

Visvanathan, K., R. Chlebowski, P. Hurley, N. Col, M. Ropka, D. Collyar, M. Morrow, et al. (2009). "American Society of Clinical Oncology Clinical Practice Guideline Update on the Use of Pharmacologic Interventions Including Tamoxifen, Raloxifene, and Aromatase Inhibition for Breast Cancer Risk Reduction." *Journal of Clinical Oncology*, 27, 3235–3258.

Wald, A. (1950). *Statistical Decision Functions*. New York: Wiley.

Wasserstein, R., and N. Lazar (2016). "The ASA's Statement on p-Values: Context, Process, and Purpose." *American Statistician* 70, 129–133.

Wennberg, J. (2011). "Time to Tackle Unwarranted Variations in Practice." *BMJ*, 342, March 26, 687–690.

Wong, S., M. Faries, E. Kennedy, S. Agarwala, T. Akhurst, C. Ariyan, C. Balch, et al. (2017). "Sentinel Lymph Node Biopsy and Management of Regional Lymph Nodes in Melanoma: American Society of Clinical Oncology and Society of Surgical Oncology Clinical Practice Guideline Update." *Journal of Clinical Oncology*, http://ascopubs.org/doi/full/10.1200/JCO .2017.75.7724.

INDEX

A NOTE ON THE TYPE

This book has been composed in Adobe Text and Gotham.
Adobe Text, designed by Robert Slimbach for Adobe,
bridges the gap between fifteenth- and sixteenth-century
calligraphic and eighteenth-century Modern styles.
Gotham, inspired by New York street signs, was designed
by Tobias Frere-Jones for Hoefler & Co.